Bobby Orr: Fire on Ice

About the Book

Ask any hockey fan who is the sport's all-time great player and he'll probably tell you Bobby Orr. Superb skater, keen strategist, aggressively offensive defenseman—Orr has led the Boston Bruins from the cellar to the stars. Along the way he won just about every hockey award in existence. In this book popular sportswriter Al Hirshberg tells the fascinating story behind this peaceable, thoughtful, friendly man. He shows how a boy in a small Canadian town became one of the flashiest and most spectacular superstars in professional hockey history.

BOBBY ORR
Fire on Ice

by Al Hirshberg

G. P. Putnam's Sons New York

To my grandson, Eric Marandett,
a young, avid hockey fan

Contents

Bobby Orr: Fire on Ice

1 Triumph of a Superstar

On May 10, 1970, a capacity crowd of 14,835 wildly enthusiastic Boston Bruins fans crammed Boston Garden to the rafters. They hoped, prayed, and yelled for a victorious climax of a magnificent hockey season for their favorites.

The idea of the Bruins failing to win the Stanley Cup was absurd. The only question was whether they would win it at home. They could by beating the St. Louis Blues on that May afternoon, for they had already won the first 3 games of a best-4-out-of-7 series. But if the Blues won, the series would return to St. Louis, and the home fans might not be in on the kill.

The Bruins themselves were just as eager as their rabid followers. They had finished second to the Chicago Black Hawks in the Eastern Division of regular season play, but then they virtually blew the Hawks off the ice by whipping them in four straight in the Stanley Cup semifinals.

That was really the big hurdle. Once over it, the Bruins would coast to the ancient mug emblematic of the championship of the National Hockey League. For, good as the Blues

11

were, they had no chance. True, they had won everything in their own division, but it was an expansion group of teams, and no expansion team can beat an outstanding established club in any sport after only three years of existence.

The Bruins *were* outstanding—there was no doubt of that. The team that Milt Schmidt had gathered together and Harry Sinden coached was the best in hockey.

And the man who made it so was a twenty-two-year-old genius named Bobby Orr.

Despite his tender years this remarkable young man was already a veteran of four years of National Hockey League play. No youth of eighteen had ever come into the league with more praise, more fanfare, or greater expectations. And no youth of eighteen had ever lived up to such praise, fanfare, and expectations.

For Bobby Orr was an instant superstar—the only one of his age hockey had ever known. Indeed, few sports had ever seen an athlete comparable to Bobby Orr, combining extreme youth with fantastic ability and poise.

Throughout his career, his only problem had been injuries, hardly unusual in the fastest, most dangerous major professional team sport in the world. Even in those first four years, he had been forced out of action time and again by injuries resulting from the bruising contact of hockey.

But not in the season nearing its close that warm May afternoon in 1970. That year, Orr had not missed a single game of regular-season play.

Coincidentally he had won virtually every honor available to a major-league hockey player. Furthermore, he made history as a defenseman, setting records which, if they ever are equaled or surpassed, will probably be by Bobby Orr himself.

His 87 assists set an all-time record for all NHL players.

His 120 points made him the first defenseman ever to lead the league in scoring, and was only 6 points short of the record set the previous year by his teammate, Phil Esposito.

He was the first man to sweep 4 major NHL trophies. He won the Norris for being the league's best defenseman. He won the Hart for being the league's Most Valuable Player. He won the Ross for leading the league in scoring. And he won the Smythe for being the Most Valuable Player in the Stanley Cup play-offs.

As he had throughout the Stanley Cup play-offs of 1970, Orr dominated the fourth game of the finals. He dominated play in every game in which he took part, for he had a charisma on the ice unprecedented by any previous NHL superstar.

"Watch Bobby Orr and you see the hockey game," was the slogan all over the league. Its accuracy was unquestioned. A newcomer to hockey had only to keep his eyes on Orr and he would indeed see virtually the whole game.

On that May afternoon in Boston the Blues proved particularly tough opponents for the Bruins. Although they had lost the first 3 games without putting up too much of a battle, they seemed determined not to let the Bruins sweep the series.

The result was a standoff at the end of the 3 regulation periods—a 3–3 tie. In season play, NHL games that were tied at the end of 3 periods went into the record books as ties. The league rules gave 2 points for a victory and 1 for a tie, with division championships decided on a total point basis.

But in Stanley Cup play-offs the tie rule did not apply. If the game were deadlocked after 3 periods, it continued into overtime periods on a "sudden death" basis. The first team to score won the game.

This was the situation in Boston that day. After a brief

rest the teams moved into overtime. If neither scored after one overtime period, they rested, then played a second, then a third, until one team scored.

Sitting in the stands behind the Bruins bench was Teddy Green, recovering from a horrible accident that had brought him to the very brink of death. In a preseason exhibition game in Ottawa, Green, a veteran member of the Bruins and one of the club's four assistant captains—the others were Johnny Bucyk, Phil Esposito, and Eddie Westfall— had suffered a depressed skull fracture after being hit over the head by a rival's hockey stick.

After many agonizing weeks in an Ottawa hospital Green had gone home to Winnipeg to recuperate. Now, still not completely recovered but well enough to travel, the veteran Bruin was in the Boston Garden as a guest of the club.

As his mates skated off the ice following the third regulation period, Green remarked, "Wouldn't it be great to win the Stanley Cup in overtime?"

Later, as the overtime period began, Green added, "It would be even better if Bobby scored the winning goal."

"He'll do it," somebody said. "You watch."

Everyone in the Garden watched. As the overtime period began, the Bruins' Derek Sanderson won the face-off and shot the puck into the Blues' zone, where Blues goalie Glenn Hall slid warily from side to side in front of his goal. Then Bobby Orr moved in.

Most defensemen do exactly what their name implies— defend. Their primary job is to keep the opposition from taking any shots on goal. Orr, as he was with everything else, was a master at it.

That, however, was about the only thing he had in common with other defensemen. Once most other defensemen had cleared the puck out of the zone, they trailed the play. If their mates took the puck into the opposition's defending

14

area, the majority of defensemen assumed positions just inside their opponents' blue line, where they tried to keep the puck inside the zone.

Sometimes, Orr *did* pass to a teammate. This was usually when he was boxed in so thoroughly that he couldn't get out. But more often he took the puck out himself, picked up one or two mates on the way, and became part of an attacking line.

This was one of his great assets. He was a fourth forward while still handling his job on defense. He succeeded at both because he was faster, cleverer, and had better control of the puck than any forward in hockey. When Orr had the puck, he was a potential scorer or playmaker. No other defenseman in the history of professional hockey—not even the legendary Eddie Shore, himself a Bruins' immortal—could compare with Orr in this respect.

When Shore, known as the "Edmonton Express" after the Canadian city in which he grew up, carried the puck from one end of the ice to the other, he would pull roaring Boston fans right to their feet. Because of the rules then in effect, which kept the defending team out of the offensive zone when not in possession of the puck, Shore had a clear field all the way up to his own blue line. By the time he had skated unmolested around behind his own net to gather speed, he was going full tilt long before reaching center ice.

Orr didn't have this advantage. When he came along, rules changes made long before permitted defenders to stay in the offensive zone after losing the puck. Thus, they could do anything legally possible to prevent the puck-carrier from taking it out.

Unlike Shore, Bobby Orr had to fight his way through the opposition even if he picked up the puck behind his own net. Without the clear field Shore always had, Orr had to use not only speed, but strength and guile in his own zone as well as everywhere else on the ice. Another of Orr's amazing assets was his ability to reach full speed in two steps. Nobody in hockey history had ever been so quick to get up a full head of steam.

And nobody in hockey history was better at finding ways to move the puck out of danger and into the opposing zone. An excellent faker, he could also change speed and direction so fast that nobody could catch him from behind.

As Teddy Green once said, "Bobby is never slow. He just has about twenty different rates of fast."

If he couldn't take the puck out himself, Orr usually got it out by passing it to a forward. Then, with his great speed, he caught up to his teammates in time to help work the puck up the ice by passing it back and forth.

In four years no one had been able to find a sure way of stopping him, except when he was having a bad night, which happened once in a while.

But not during those 1970 play-offs. As that fourth game of the finals against the Blues moved into its overtime period, Orr had scored 19 points—8 goals and 11 assists. That was already a record for defensemen in play-off games.

The Blues, with everyone else, were scared to death of him, as well they might be. They agreed with Harry Sinden's analysis of Orr's magnificent talents.

"I'd hate to have to figure out how to check Orr," Sinden once said. "I don't think it can be done.

"If you go into our zone with him," the Bruins coach added, "he starts so fast he'll leave you there. If you wait for him at the blue or red line, he'll blow right past you or pass the puck by you. The fact that Orr's a defenseman makes it even tougher. If you put a man on him, you'd have to leave one of your forwards open, and Orr is such a great playmaker he'd surely get the puck to the open man."

Boston Garden was in an uproar as the seconds of the

overtime period ticked by. The crowd seemed to sense that this was the crucial point when the Bruins would clinch the Stanley Cup.

Not since 1941, nearly thirty years before, had they won the ancient cup that means so much in hockey. Bruins fans, hungry for the championship that had eluded their favorites in all those intervening years, were eager for a victory.

"Bobby will do it," murmured teammates on the bench.

"Bobby will do it," cried fans from the stands.

"Bobby will do it," thought Bruins players on the ice.

Everything was Bobby—Bobby—Bobby. After the play-offs ended even the Blues admitted they were trying not to face something that seemed certain—that Bobby *would* do it, if not in this overtime period, then in the next, or in any subsequent overtime period that might have to be played.

One man had no intention of seeing the play-offs last longer than that fourth game, or that game last longer than one overtime, or that overtime last longer than the few seconds it might take to get the puck on his stick near the Blues goal.

That man was Bobby Orr.

When the Bruins got possession of the puck, Bobby took control.

He swept down the ice, his head up, his stick at the ready. When Sanderson shot the puck in the zone, Orr sped in, blocking the puck inside the blue line. As Sanderson skated behind the net, Orr passed the puck around the boards to him and moved out in front of the net. With defenseman Jean Guy Talbot between them, Sanderson flipped the puck deftly over Talbot's stick back to Orr. Bobby slapped the puck quickly, and it whizzed between Hall's right leg and arm and into the net.

Boston won its first Stanley Cup in twenty-nine years in exactly forty seconds of overtime play.

As Orr lifted his stick in the traditional triumphant hockey gesture to indicate a goal, his teammates nearest him threw their arms around him and nearly carried him back to the bench.

And from the Bruins bench poured the rest of his teammates, from Harry Sinden down, all headed for the amazing youth who had crowned an incredible season with its most important goal.

Standing behind the bench, tears pouring down his weatherbeaten face, Terry Green, the injured Bruin star, could do nothing but marvel, as he had so often, at the light-haired youth who had done what all Bruins and Bruins fans hoped for—he had scored the winning goal in Boston to win the Stanley Cup.

With that goal Bobby Orr completed a remarkable feat. In every one of the 14 play-off games in which the Bruins had played he had scored at least 1 point. That goal, his ninth of the play-offs and his twentieth point, put his offensive record even farther out of reach for future defensemen.

It was a remarkable display of clutch hockey, the kind that usually happens only in storybooks. But that was nothing new to Orr. He was a storybook hockey player, a man who by himself had already helped lift the sport to a special place in the hearts of American fans, into a niche beside baseball, football, and basketball.

Before Orr's time hockey was Canada's national pastime, comparatively little-known elsewhere except in parts of Europe and in the four American cities with teams in the National Hockey League.

Expansion and television had brought hockey into American homes.

Bobby Orr had kept it there.

His winning goal, which gave the Bruins a sweep of the finals over the St. Louis Blues, did not simply win the

Stanley Cup. Coming as it did in overtime, with two nations watching it on television, it completed Boston's triumph at home. It meant that Boston fans could share a victory they might otherwise have had to watch on television.

The man who made it possible was Bobby Orr.

He had done exactly what was expected of him. He had scored the goal everyone thought he would score, at the time it meant the most.

That goal, in overtime, had finished the series.

It was only fitting that Orr score it. Nobody else could have given it the same meaning.

At twenty-two, this youth, whose hair was blonder than brown, browner than blond, and whose handsome face was soon to become known the world over, was the bona fide king of his chosen profession.

It seemed impossible that any others, anywhere, could be happier for him than the Boston hockey fans.

But there were others, somewhere else.

His family, his friends, in fact, the entire community of Parry Sound, Ontario.

It was there that Bobby Orr had been born, there that he had grown up, and there that he had learned to play hockey as no boy had ever played it before.

Boston Garden was a long way from Parry Sound. The Boston Bruins were a far cry from the kid teams Bobby Orr played on as a child in the small, well-known summer resort in Ontario. Now, because of Bobby Orr, no one would ever forget it in the winter.

2 Parry Sound

Parry Sound, Ontario, is a friendly town of about six thousand some one hundred and forty-five miles north of Toronto. Extremely cold weather is a way of life, just as it is practically everywhere else in Canada during the winter. In Parry Sound the temperature sometimes drops to forty degrees below zero, with the ice on nearby Georgian Bay occasionally three feet thick.

For a growing boy who loves sports, ice hockey is the most natural thing in the world in Parry Sound. Bobby Orr, the third of Doug and Arva Orr's five children, was skating as soon as he could walk. This was not unusual. Practically every father in town put a young son on skates when the boy was hardly out of his baby shoes.

Doug Orr had a special interest in hockey, for he had once had a chance to play professionally himself. At sixteen, he was skating on the same forward line with Pete Horeck in Canadian Junior hockey when the Boston Bruins approached him. Doug was ready to sign when he learned the Bruins intended to send him to their farm club in Atlantic City, so he refused their offer and went into the Canadian navy instead.

Horeck, who did sign a professional contract, went on to play for several years in the National Hockey League. But, not being particularly outstanding, comparatively few noticed him, and, except for some veteran hockey scouts, none realized that he and Bobby Orr's father had been teammates in junior hockey.

Doug came by his athletic ability naturally, for *his* father, Robert Orr, for whom Bobby was named, had been a professional soccer player in Ireland before emigrating to Canada. Thus, Bobby was a third-generation athlete of quality. That his abilities far outweighed both those of his father and his grandfather was not unusual. Most unusual, however, was his age when those great abilities began to emerge.

For, strange though it seems, Bobby Orr was an outstanding hockey player at the age of eight. By the time he was ten he was better than boys fourteen or fifteen. From then on, he always played with older and bigger boys—not only played with them but consistently outstripped them.

Not that Bobby was a one-sport athlete. In 1939, nine years before Bobby was born, his father had been voted the outstanding athlete in a Parry Sound high school track meet. Years later, when Bobby was in high school, he won the very same trophy.

But hockey was his game and, even at eight years old, his obvious future. A graceful skater before he was in the first grade, he did everything else expected of a hockey player before he was out of grammar school.

"I remember watching him when he was three," Doug once said. "He'd take a stride, fall on his face, get up, and keep on skating."

He may have cried when he fell on his face, but he didn't rush into his father's arms for solace. The principal thing in Doug Orr's recollection of Bobby at three was not that he fell, but that he *got up and kept on skating.*

22

Although far superior to others on the ice, Bobby was always modest and friendly. Even when he was playing hockey with boys much older, he had friends of his own age, with whom he did all the things a youngster might do in a town like Parry Sound.

When the weather was warm, he went fishing and skinny-dipping with his pals and to this day loves to hunt and fish. He knew the forests around Georgian Bay as well as his own backyard—in fact, they *were* his backyard. The bay itself was his swimming pool as well as his hockey rink.

Nobody ever had to urge Bobby to play hockey. Unlike some fathers whose athletic hopes were never fulfilled, Doug Orr let hockey come naturally to his talented young son. Bobby himself has no memory of learning to skate. Nor, for that matter, is he sure who taught him the hockey moves that today mystify his National Hockey League rivals.

Everything in hockey came as naturally to him as if he had been born with a stick in his hand.

Actually he did the rest himself, not because he had to, but because he wanted to. Not until he was in junior hockey did he have to learn consciously what should or should not be done.

"He could have taught his elders some of the fine points of hockey," an old Parry Sound friend once said of him. "At ten and eleven and twelve, he was making moves astonishingly like the moves he makes today."

Hockey is not an easy game to learn, and the best hockey players need instruction somewhere along the line. All Bobby Orr ever needed was maturity, experience, and a few tips here and there.

In Canada organized hockey begins at an early age. A youngster of eight is old enough to join the smallest of the groups, and the ambition of all young boys who like hockey is to play in the Juniors. To reach that level, a boy must move up through the ranks in accordance with his age.

Most boys did, but not Bobby Orr. He always outgrew his age group—not in size, but in ability. When at the Pee-wee age, he was playing Bantam class. He skipped the Midget class altogether, for when he was at that age, he was already playing Junior A. When he first broke in with the Bruins in 1966, he was eighteen years old, the age of an average Junior in the Canadian system.

Even after he became rich and famous, Bobby was always an Orr, a proud member of a proud and close-knit family. Both of his parents were Parry Sounders through and through—born and raised there. So were Pat, his older sister, Ron, his older brother, Penny, his younger sister, and the family baby, Doug, Jr.

Where one was, they all were. This included Bobby's earliest days in organized hockey. Wherever he played, everyone in the family was there to see him. After young Doug was born the seven Orrs were a familiar sight wherever Bobby played. They all piled into a car and drove off— sometimes more than one hundred miles from Parry Sound.

Doug Orr was not rich, but he always had a good job. He and his family lived in a nine-room house on Great North Road, where they live to this day. During one period, when Bobby was about ten, his father worked nights so that he could watch Bobby play after school during the days.

Later Doug became packing supervisor of the Parry Sound plant of Canadian Industries, Limited, manufacturers of high explosives, specializing in dynamite. For years after Bobby was making big money out of hockey, Doug was still working there, for he is a proud man with no desire to take advantage of his son's amazing earning power.

His only concession to Bobby's fame was a willingness to retire a little earlier than he had intended—in 1973, in fact. By then, Bobby, with all his outside interests to augment his professional hockey contract, was very close to being a millionaire. His wealth didn't change him. At that point in his life, he was still going home to Parry Sound to spend most of the off-season with his family.

Single-handedly, Bobby made Parry Sound the sort of Canadian shrine the Dionne quintuplets made their town of Callander, Ontario. Tourists who had never heard of the place before Bobby became well-known went out of their way to drive through there. Some even stopped at the Orr home in hopes of seeing or talking to Bobby.

At twelve, Bobby was with a Parry Sound Bantam team sponsored by the Macklaim Construction Company. His coach was Wilfred "Bucko" McDonald, former NHL defenseman, who ran the minor-hockey program in Parry Sound. Although two years younger than the other Bantams, he was one of the cleverest players on his team. He was "deking" opposing hockey players then: faking one direction, pulling rivals over, then changing direction and moving away so fast that he repeatedly left behind a bewildered opposition. He was the fastest skater on the ice in every game he played.

"Bobby was always an excellent skater," his father recalled. "And I wasn't the only one who noticed it. From the time he was eight everyone watching him commented on his grace and speed."

He needed only to grow up. An eight-year-old among twelve-year-olds looks like a midget, and Bobby was no exception. But even then he could outplay the older boys. And as he grew older, he continued to dominate the ice.

When the Parry Sound Bantams went to an Ontario minor-hockey league play-off in the town of Gananoque, Ontario, the Bantams were not the principal attraction of the tournament; they were only another group of young players to take part in events featuring professionals.

Naturally the professional teams drew the largest crowds, as well as scouts from various National Hockey League teams. Not many people were watching the Bantams except relatives and friends of the players, including, of course, all the Orrs.

The Boston Bruins, who had spent years looking for a superstar to spark their team out of the doldrums, were yet to find the man they needed. They wanted another Bobby Hull, or a Gordie Howe, or a Jean Beliveau—someone around whom they could build a championship team.

Their owner, Weston Adams, Sr., whose father, Charles F. Adams, had founded the Bruins and introduced the National Hockey League to the United States, went with his general manager, Lynn Patrick, his assistant general manager, Milt Schmidt, and others on the Bruins staff to Gananoque in 1960. They visited the town, about the size of Parry Sound and on the St. Lawrence Seaway, specifically to watch two potential Junior A hockey players on the Gananoque team, one named Higgins, the other Eaton.

Both players had signed Bruins contracts. They were playing for the Kingston Frontenacs in the Eastern Professional League. Their coach was a young man named Wren Blair, who years later became general manager of the Minnesota North Stars, when it was one of the National Hockey League's expansion teams.

Then twelve years old, Bobby Orr, as usual, was a runt among giants. Only an inch over five feet tall, this sixth grader would have been taken for the team mascot off the ice. Far and away its smallest player, wearing hockey pants so big for him they came down below his knees, he hardly seemed strong enough to hold a stick.

Indeed, in those days that was Bobby's only weakness. He could compete artistically, but not physically, with the older, bigger, stronger boys with and against whom he played.

But since hockey is a contact sport, there was no way Bobby could wrestle down a fourteen-year-old rival in a hand-to-hand fight. What he lacked in strength he made up for in courage and guile, but he simply wasn't big enough to fight off boys several inches taller and many pounds heavier.

Even this shortcoming could not eclipse Bobby's natural class as a hockey player. Nobody on the ice at Gananoque that day the Bruins' brass went to see a couple of their prospects had the flair and the style of the little boy from Parry Sound.

"It was a strange thing," Blair recalled later. "We're at this game watching Higgins and Eaton on one rink, yet every one of us was aware that on another a little boy on the Parry Sound team was dominating his game. Every time I looked he had the puck and was hustling down the ice with it. And every move I saw him make seemed to be the right one."

Afterward Blair said to Lynn Patrick, "How do you like our kids?"

"Not bad," Patrick said.

"See anyone else you liked?"

Patrick looked at him, smiled, and said, "Do you mean number two in that Bantam game?"

"That's just who I mean," Blair said.

Number two in the Bantam game was Bobby Orr. The contingent of hockey men from Boston nearly forgot all about Higgins and Eaton. (Neither ever made it to the National Hockey League.) All they could talk about was the smallest boy on an amateur team from a little community on Georgian Bay.

Blair Wren was the only man in the Bruins' party in Canada almost all the time. Patrick designated him to stop in Parry Sound whenever possible to keep an eye on Bobby Orr.

27

From then on, Wren always made it a point to take his Kingston team into Parry Sound for the pregame meal when the team went on the road. Sometimes it meant going many miles out of the way, but Wren knew the detour was worthwhile.

For some time the people of the town couldn't understand why a professional team stopped there so often, then went on to play elsewhere. The reason was Wren's desire to stop in on the Orrs, get to know Bobby and his family, and set the stage for him to join the Bruins.

These stops were necessary because the Boston people were not the only professional hockey men to notice the little guy from Parry Sound at that play-off in Gananoque. Scouts and officials from the other National Hockey League teams were just as impressed with Bobby as the Bruins were.

Obviously there would be a scramble for his services when the time came. Nobody could think of signing a twelve-year-old. But it would only take a few years for him to become the object of every team in hockey.

In those days there was no age limit for signing young prospects. Today, a boy can't be signed by an NHL team until he is twenty. In addition the NHL now has a draft system similar to other professional sports, which it didn't have then. On all prospects, the team that finishes lowest in the standings one year·gets the choice of young players for the year following, and each team gets the following choices, working in reverse order of the standings.

Bobby was nowhere near old enough to play Junior hockey when Wren first began dropping in at his house. However, Wren was sure he was ready. Once he began stopping at Parry Sound, he learned when Bobby would play, and he started going out with Doug to watch him.

"I wanted to see if the kid was really that good," Wren said years later. "Watching him at close range made me sure he was even better than we thought. Except for his size, I actually think he could have played Junior hockey at twelve."

Badly as he wanted Bobby to play professional hockey, Doug was too good a father to let him start too soon. It was two years before he made the decision that sealed Bobby's future.

In those two years the whole big-league hockey world learned all about Bobby. Before he was fourteen, scouts from all six of the NHL clubs were going to Parry Sound periodically for the sole purpose of watching him play and meeting his father, the man who would make the final decision.

But none had the advantage Blair Wren had built up. Wren had been the first professional hockey man to make it his business to know the Orrs, not just Bobby and his father, but everyone in the family.

It was many years before the day of big bonuses for signing hockey contracts, but the Bruins were prepared to do whatever might be necessary in order to sign Bobby. They would have subsidized Parry Sound's whole hockey program if they had had to.

Wren was most realistic about the situation. "To begin with," he said, "I didn't have to try too hard to be nice to the Orrs. They're just nice people, and I sincerely liked them all. And I respected their solidarity. They are truly a one-for-all, all-for-one family.

"But from a professional standpoint," he added, "it was always a fact that if you wanted the boy, you had to get to know his parents. It's not who sees him first, but who signs him that counts. Salesmanship is most important. You've got to go into those living rooms if you want a young player badly enough."

In 1962, when Bobby was fourteen years old and in the eighth grade, Blair and Doug Orr came to an agreement.

Bobby was to play for the Bruins' Junior team at Oshawa, Ontario, in return for a package worth a total of $2,700.

This included a thousand dollars in cash, a used car worth nine hundred dollars for Doug, and a new eight-hundred-dollar stucco job on the Orrs' home.

It was one of the greatest bargains in modern professional sports. The Bruins got the finest all-around hockey player in the game's history for a total of less than $3,000.

And even though Bobby was only fourteen, they all knew they had that potential superstar they had been looking for so long.

Bobby Orr at fourteen was no superstar. But within a few years, he would begin to equal the Gordie Howes, the Bobby Hulls, and the Jean Beliveaus of professional hockey fame.

And if injuries did not stop him, it was a sure bet the day would come when Bobby Orr would top them all.

3 Oshawa

To understand how the Boston Bruins could sign Bobby Orr to a contract at the tender age of fourteen, it is necessary to understand the whole system of signing professional hockey players before the National Hockey League adopted the draft system.

At that time there was no age limit. There was also an informal territorial understanding, whereby the six teams in the league got first choice of the young players within their geographical orbit. This gave the Montreal Canadiens and the Toronto Maple Leafs a tremendous advantage over the other four clubs, all of which were in the United States.

Except for Detroit, none was near the Canadian border. Boston, New York, and Chicago had few, if any, promising young hockey players within their orbits. They had to rely on their scouts to pick up boys where they could find them anywhere in Canada. Montreal and Toronto, surrounded by youngsters playing on natural ice right in the cities, didn't have that problem. They could find much of the material they wanted within streetcar range.

Territorial preferences enjoyed particularly by Toronto

and Montreal didn't necessarily mean that every hockey player in the area around those cities had to go to the Leafs or the Canadiens. The other teams scouted in their territories, but the pickings were pretty slim. Most of the good players had already been signed up.

But Parry Sound was too far from Toronto to be within its territorial orbit. How the Detroit Red Wings scout missed Bobby Orr is a puzzle to this day. The boy was a local celebrity at the age of twelve. The Bruins' acquisition of Orr was a very lucky break.

Orr wasn't the youngest ever to sign with a big-league hockey organization, but he was the youngest the Bruins ever signed. Milt Schmidt, star, coach, assistant general manager, and eventually general manager of the Bruins, had signed with the Bruins at fifteen. He became one of the greatest centers of all time.

One problem in signing young boys was their schooling. The Orrs were very much concerned about Bobby's education, and the fact that, since Parry Sound had no Junior A team, Bobby would have to play elsewhere.

The Bruins assigned him to their Oshawa farm team in the Ontario Hockey Association Junior A League. This was technically an amateur team, as Junior A hockey always has been in Canada. However, it was generally accepted that the next step up the ladder was the NHL.

Even today, with several more minor hockey leagues than there were in 1962, when Bobby signed his contract, Junior A is very fast hockey in Canada. However, since the age limit for NHL contracts is twenty, Junior A players are usually ready at least for the minor leagues, which is where most of them go after being chosen in the professional draft.

To make sure that Orr would not feel lost among men much older than he, the Bruins transfered Wren from Kingston to Oshawa. This was not a demotion, although Wren had been coaching professionals. On the contrary, it was a tribute to his ability and his close friendship with Bobby and his family.

Neither of Bobby's parents wanted him to live away from home yet, so during his first couple of years with Oshawa they drove back and forth from Parry Sound. It was a long commute, but the only way they could keep Bobby living and going to school at home while playing at Oshawa. He was starting the eighth grade when the Bruins signed him. He finished it at Parry Sound.

On the day he reported to Oshawa for the first time, Orr weighed just 125 pounds. As he stood on the ice for a roll call of all the candidates he seemed buried in the group of men, some of whom were a head taller. Each man had to answer when his name was called and announce his position. When Wren called out, "Orr," Bobby stepped forward, repeated his name and said, "Defense."

The whole squad, including Wren and Bobby, himself, exploded with laughter. Defensemen were supposed to be big and rugged. Here was the smallest, lightest, youngest boy on the team. How he could compete for a defense job with others so much bigger was a mystery only Bobby could solve.

And solve it he did. In the first skating sessions he was obviously the best and fastest man on the ice. When the squad was split up into teams, he took complete control of the scrimmages. He played defense not by hitting oncoming forwards, but by stealing the puck from them and flying down the ice, or by tying them up so that they couldn't get rid of it.

Once again, as with the Parry Sound Bantams, Bobby proved that what he lacked in size he made up for in savvy and courage. Despite his size, he wasn't afraid of being hit.

33

In fact, he was so elusive that few men ever really hit him. They couldn't keep up with him.

Red Fisher, the columnist and hockey expert of the Montreal *Star,* was one of the first newspaper reporters to see him play Junior A hockey. Some years later, he wrote in *Sport* magazine:

"Those who know Bobby Orr say he never was a boy. He was making the same moves at fourteen that he makes now."

He was a boy surrounded by young men and outplaying them all. Even Wren, who knew him so well, marveled at his ability to play by nature a game so hard to learn.

Oshawa had a good, but not great team. Without Bobby it would have been just another club in the league. With him it was a contender for the league championship.

During his first year on the club, Bobby scored 14 goals. To see this little guy flying down the ice, often all alone because his teammates couldn't keep up with him, was in itself a rare pleasure for a hockey fan.

To see him get past big, strong defensemen, mostly by faking them out of position, was more than a pleasure. It was a memorable experience.

And to see him beat goalies, taller, heavier and stronger, was a real thrill. Never had even Junior A hockey seen his equal. The great pros of the past may have been as good, but none were as young. A fourteen-year-old had no business making monkeys out of youths upwards of twenty, but Bobby Orr did it regularly.

He not only played conventional hockey better than anyone else in the league, but he made unconventional, well-nigh impossible, moves.

In his second year at Oshawa, when he was fifteen years old, Bobby, in a game against the Toronto Marlboros, pulled one of the most amazing stunts Wren or anyone else had ever seen.

Late in the game, with Oshawa trailing by a goal, Wren pulled out his goalie in favor of a sixth skater. Any time this is done, it is a desperation maneuver carrying with it an obvious risk. If an opposing player gains control of the puck and gets clear, he has an open net to shoot at.

It happened in that game. Jim McKenny of the Marlboros, who later played for the Maple Leafs, got loose and headed toward the Oshawa goal. While he was working himself clear of the crush of players in his own zone, Orr dashed madly toward his own unprotected net. By the time McKenny had a shot on the goal Orr was skating backward, but still far short of his goal.

McKenny let a shot go that seemed headed straight for Oshawa's goal. At the last instant, Bobby threw himself at the puck, making a miraculous stop.

The play had no effect on the outcome, since it was too late for Oshawa to score, but no one who saw it could believe his eyes.

That was the way it always was with Orr. He did things in Junior A hockey that, considering his age, were little miracles. And, of course, as he grew older, the little miracles became big ones.

The only thing he ever needed was experience, and he got four years of it at Oshawa. The Bruins were in trouble all through that period, but they had no intention of trying to rush Orr to Boston before he was ready.

He made the league's second All-Star team during that first year at Oshawa. The next year, when he was fifteen, he scored 29 goals and made the first All-Star team.

In his third year at Oshawa he scored 34 goals and had 59 assists, a total of 93 points in 56 games. That was a league record for defensemen.

He finished his career at Oshawa in the 1965–66 season

with 38 goals. By that time he had filled out to nearly six feet and 185 pounds and was captain of the Oshawa team.

Wren handled him as well as the Bruins expected him to. He gave Bobby his head, let him carry the puck whenever he could, and encouraged him to lead attacks, even though he was a defenseman.

Orr led the team to the finals of the Memorial Cup playoffs for the Junior championship of Canada. But in a previous series he had suffered a groin injury that threatened to keep him out of action.

Oshawa was playing Edmonton for the title. Doug Orr and the family were among those present to see Bobby finish up the most glittering Junior career Canada had ever known. As they sat in the locker room, Hap Emms, then general manager of the Bruins, came in to tell Orr he was out of the game.

"We can't take a chance of ruining your career at this stage," Emms said.

As Emms turned to leave, Bobby waited until he was out of earshot, then said to his father, "Boy, I wish he hadn't said that. This is my last game and I really wanted to be in it."

"Can you play without aggravating the injury?" Doug said.

"Look, Dad," said Bobby, "what difference does it make? The season's over after today. I'm the captain of the team, we've got a chance for the cup and I'll never have another chance like it. You have no idea what this game means to me."

"Yes, I have," Doug said.

He followed Emms out of the locker room, and they met in the corridor.

"Bobby wants to play," he said.

"Well," Emms said, "I don't want him to."

"You don't own the boy yet," Doug said. "I'm his father and I say he'll play."

And that was that. Bobby played, but Edmonton, the strongest team in Canada, won the title. Bobby was hampered and in pain from the injury. He did play briefly in the first two games, sat out game three, played again briefly in the fifth and most of the sixth game. His movements were restricted, but he insisted on playing.

It is probable that few, if any, Canadian Junior players ever had the advance publicity in a big-league city that Bobby Orr had in Boston, especially during his final year at Oshawa.

The Bruins were just completing the seventh straight season in which they failed to make the Stanley Cup playoffs. Boston, which had always been hockey-mad, loved them as much as ever, but the fans there were tired of seeing them suffer constant defeat.

In order to give them a lift the Bruins, who had publicized Orr here and there in previous years, really went all out during his fourth Junior A season. They sent occasional bulletins to the Boston media, and soon Orr was nearly as well known to Boston fans as the Bruins players themselves.

Because of Bobby's speed and his terrific shot—as hard as anyone's in the NHL by the time he was eighteen—the Bruins brass thought seriously about making him a center. At the direction of his bosses, Blair played Orr at center a few times in Junior A hockey, but strongly advised against trying to make the move permanent.

There were several reasons, not the least of which was that Bobby himself didn't want to shift.

"I feel more in the game on defense," he once said. "You can see everything that goes on from there, and can be better prepared to take the puck in whenever the chance comes. In fact, you can see chances develop.

37

"But when you're playing center, you're always up the ice where the only thing you know is what you and your wings are doing. And when the other team gets the puck, you have to check back all the time. Besides, I miss the challenge of stopping opposing forwards when they come at me with the puck. You miss all of that as a center."

When he first played with the Bruins, they also tried moving him to center. He did so well that some observers said that even at his age—he was eighteen then—he probably could develop into the game's best center before the end of the season.

There was little doubt about the truth of the statement. Orr *could* become the best center in hockey. He could become the best wing, and already appeared to be the best defenseman. It was not impossible that he could even become the best goalie if he set his mind to it.

But the Bruins didn't shift him to center because it wasn't necessary. From his defense position he could make all the moves of a great center whenever he wanted to. And as a defenseman, he could do double duty. He could protect his own zone and, whenever the occasion arose, move the puck into the opposing team's zone.

Milt Schmidt put it all in a nutshell when he said, "Why move the best defenseman in hockey to center, especially when he is such an offensive-minded defenseman?"

Schmidt knew what he was talking about. While in the prime of his own career he had played on the same team with Eddie Shore. Before Orr came along, Shore was the most offensive-minded defenseman hockey had ever known.

4 Orr and Shore

When Bobby Orr first joined the Bruins, the easiest way for a modern fan to get into an argument with an old-timer was to say that Orr was a better hockey player than Eddie Shore.

It is the way of veteran sports followers in general to insist that the heroes of their day were better than today's heroes. This is especially so when the discussion concerns superstars. Eddie Shore was a superstar. And from the moment he joined the Bruins, so was Bobby Orr.

There is a legend that when Charles F. Adams founded the Boston Bruins, he bought the entire Western Hockey League just to get Eddie Shore. It wasn't true, although many senior hockey fans around Boston still believe it.

Actually Shore wasn't even a defenseman when the Bruins got him. He was a bruising, fast forward, more famous for his toughness than for anything else. He wasn't a great skater; in those days he didn't have to be.

When the Bruins bought the Western Hockey League from Lester Patrick and his brother, Frank (Lester was the father of Lynn Patrick, later the Bruins' general manager),

39

Shore was only one of more than a dozen outstanding hockey players.

They were all of such fine quality that the National Hockey League president at that time, Frank Calder (for whom the Calder Trophy for the league's outstanding rookie was named), made Adams sell at least two-thirds of them.

Calder also insisted that they be evenly distributed among the other NHL teams.

If Adams, who reportedly paid more than a quarter of a million dollars for the league, had been allowed to keep everybody, the Bruins would have been so far ahead of the other teams that nobody could have caught up with them for years.

Adams kept three or four, including Shore, and made so much money selling the others that he almost came out even on the deal. The story that he bought the league only for Shore didn't begin circulating for several years, when the so-called Edmonton Express had become one of the most valuable and colorful figures in hockey.

The man who made a defenseman of Shore was Art Ross, the Bruins coach. It was Ross, a veteran hockey star and former professional motorcycle racer, who selected the men the Bruins kept and advised Adams where to sell the others.

Ross knew that Shore would be a better defenseman than a forward for several reasons: He was so rough he could stop oncoming skaters by sheer strength; although not a great skater, he was so fast and reckless that he could carry the puck the length of the ice by himself; and he had one of the greatest shots in the league.

From a tactical standpoint Shore was better on defense than at forward because he was a lone wolf on the ice. On offense he worked much better by himself than with others. He loved to shoot and hated to pass, making him an ineffective lineman.

On defense he was perfect for his time. Although he could not work with other forwards, he worked very well with a defense partner. He and Lionel Hitchman, a tall, rangy man almost as tough as Shore, were the roughest pair of defensemen in hockey. It was worth an opposing forward's neck trying to get through them.

All of which made Shore great for the era in which he played. But as an all-around hockey man, he wasn't in the same class with Bobby Orr.

People who have seen both in action feel that Shore was tougher than Orr. But Orr could be as bruising as anyone in hockey, as he had been almost since he first broke in with the Bruins in the 1966–67 season.

Fans were fooled by his early start in organized hockey. When he first played Junior A at Oshawa, he had neither the size nor the strength for the physical contact the pro game demands. But by the time he joined the Bruins, at eighteen, he was nearing his full growth. When he reached it a year or two later, he could compete physically with anyone.

Shore didn't compare with Orr as a skater. He was fast but awkward. Orr is fast and truly graceful. Shore ran on skates. Orr glides on them. Shore was all muscle and power. Orr is deceptive and clever.

Shore had a great shot but Orr has a better one. This may owe in part to the improvement of equipment since Shore's time. Shore went to the NHL in the mid-twenties, Orr in the mid-sixties. During that forty-year period, sticks, skates, protective gear, everything having to do with the game, improved.

Orr has much more to contend with than Shore did. Hockey players in general are better than in Shore's time. Even the average player can manufacture a good shot with the help of curves in the stick that weren't legal in Shore's time.

Shore benefited from old rules, which prohibited the attacking team from being in the defending zone without possession of the puck. When the attacking team lost the puck, it had to backcheck to a point beyond the blue line. Today when the attacking team loses the puck, they can stay in the defending zone while trying to get it back.

That meant that while Shore could get an unobstructed fast start by swinging around behind his own net, Orr has to fight his way up the first third of the ice.

This pointed up another prime difference between the two. Shore needed a fast start to get up to full speed. Orr can go from a standstill to full speed in two strides.

Shore was a selfish player, Orr willingly gives up the puck if he sees a teammate in a better position to score. In fact, Orr's annual output of assists in any single season was more than Shore's total for his whole career.

It's possible, but doubtful, that Shore might have adjusted to modern hockey. But he was so headstrong, so sure of himself, so stubborn, and so hard to get along with that such an adjustment would have been very difficult for him.

The personality differences between them were all to Orr's advantage. Even at his peak Orr never developed a swelled head. Except under extraordinary conditions, he was the same polite, considerate man at maturity he had been as a boy.

Shore was much the same off the ice as on—belligerent, challenging, suspicious of strangers, and generally a loner.

On the ice Orr is nearly as tough as Shore and fully as effective. Off it he is self-effacing, a friendly young man sought out by others.

Shore had few friends and Orr was everybody's friend. Shore's teammates did not like him. Orr's worshipped him. Members of the Bruins consider Orr among their best friends. If anyone were hurt badly enough to land in the hospital for any length of time, the man he was likely to hear from most often was Bobby Orr. Teddy Green comments that Orr didn't miss a week without phoning two or three times to cheer him up while Green was recovering from a depressed skull fracture suffered in a preseason exhibition game.

Personality traits may or may not mean much when a big-league hockey player is involved in the heat of a game. Sometimes it is better to be naturally mean in order to survive in the professional jungle of this furious contact game.

But Orr is mean only on the ice. Throughout his career he has never come close to winning the Lady Byng Trophy for gentlemanliness in action. He spends as much time in the penalty box every year as the average NHL player.

However, when a game is over, the heated emotions end with it. Orr can leave it all back on the ice.

Shore couldn't. He developed personal hatreds that were reflected in his play. Sometimes he even announced before a game whom he was going to "get." Orr never does, yet he is just as tough on the ice as Shore.

Because he can do everything demanded of a hockey player, Orr is *expected* to do everything. He is so thoroughly effective in every aspect of the game, and makes so many things look gracefully simple that even his warmest followers don't fully understand his amazing all-around ability. Both ice-length rushes and bone-rattling collisions are integral parts of Bobby's style. But they are only two of his many abilities—not the only things he can do.

When the contingent of Bruins officials first saw Bobby Orr at Gananoque, they were amazed at the many things Orr did naturally. When he grew up and gained experience he learned many more, for then he had the strength to cope with big rivals.

43

He is the perfect all-around hockey player, and hard-nosed as well.

Shore was hard-nosed and great in his own way, but far from perfect. There were too many hockey essentials he couldn't handle. Knowing that, he didn't try.

Orr handles them all, which is the reason he is a far better man to have on a hockey team.

But the argument will go on in Boston as long as hockey and Shore fans live. And of course, like all such arguments, it will never be settled.

Modern hockey followers are unanimous in their insistence that no greater player than Bobby Orr ever lived.

5 Highest-Paid Rookie

When Bobby signed his first Junior A contract with the Bruins at fourteen, neither he nor his father had any real idea of his worth. And, although Bobby decided when to sign, Doug did the actual negotiating.

The Orrs were at the mercy of the Bruins. There was nothing unusual about this because all hockey players—including the great ones—were at the mercy of the clubs for which they played. Until Orr came along, they were in general the most poorly paid professional athletes in the United States and Canada.

In the late fifties, for example, the hottest man in hockey was Maurice Richard of the Canadiens. At his peak Richard never made more than $25,000 a season. During the same period Ted Williams of baseball's Boston Red Sox was earning more than $100,000 a season.

The reason for the huge difference in top pay at that time was that baseball was a big television sport and hockey wasn't.

When Bobby joined the Bruins, the NHL was still a six-club league, and hockey was still considered a minor sport

45

in the United States. Of the six teams two (Toronto and Montreal) were in Canada. The four American teams were in Boston, New York, Detroit, and Chicago.

Outside those four cities most U. S. sports fans couldn't have cared less about hockey. With little or no television time and the game confined to the northeastern sector of the country, Americans elsewhere had no chance to see the NHL in action.

Minor-league hockey filled some of the gap but couldn't generate the interest big-league hockey could.

The biggest problem was the attitude of the NHL owners themselves. Because they were making so much money in each of their six cities, they were in no hurry to expand. The league had been a closed corporation for years. Why not, they reasoned, keep it that way? As long as *they* were doing so well, it made no difference to the owners if the game didn't expand to other parts of the country.

Except for the early part of the season—up to about Christmas—almost every game in every city was a solid sell-out. It was almost impossible to get tickets at any time in Montreal, Toronto, and Detroit. In Boston, Chicago, and New York, the situation was just as tight when the teams had a shot at the play-offs. Even when they didn't, these clubs also drew very well.

It was a fact, for example, that even during their leanest years—those immediately preceding the 1966–67 season, when Bobby Orr joined them—the Bruins consistently outdrew basketball's Boston Celtics.

The Celtics, although perpetual National Basketball Association champions, always played second fiddle in Boston to the last-place Bruins. This was true in media attention as well as in game attendance.

In a limited way, since so few cities were involved, the NHL was a smashing success even without television. Only when they found it was impossible to get national television coverage because only four American cities were involved did the league governors finally vote to expand in 1967.

Doug Orr had never been thoroughly satisfied with the original deal he had signed with the Bruins for Bobby. He realized he had neither demanded nor obtained enough. His lack of business knowledge had been a serious handicap in trying to talk finances with experts.

Considering Bobby's potential, Doug had, indeed, tied his son up with the Bruins for a pittance. He had made no attempt to play one NHL team off against another.

By the time Bobby signed a Bruins Junior card, all five of the other teams had tried to get him. Doug had taken the first offer that had come along. By Parry Sound standards it had seemed a good one; and at that time by ordinary hockey standards it was.

But Bobby Orr was no ordinary hockey player, even at fourteen. Doug knew that. He had been at a disadvantage because of his lack of experience in a business about which he knew nothing.

Furthermore, Doug was annoyed because, without putting anything on paper, the Bruins had informally promised to provide Bobby with some new clothes and had never got around to buying any.

On top of everything else, the Orrs got all the Boston papers during the hockey season, and, especially in Bobby's last year in Junior A, they saw their boy getting more publicity than the Bruins.

They were in the league cellar and had been for years. Obviously they expected Bobby to pull them out. Whether he succeeded or not, Doug justifiably felt the boy was worth a good deal more money than NHL rookies were normally paid.

One of the complications of the system of signing hockey

players before the NHL installed its player draft and set the age limit at twenty was that agreement to play for a Junior team did not automatically mean the player would sign for the sponsoring team.

In other words, if team and player failed to come to an agreement, it was customary to sell or trade rights to him to another NHL club.

And the contract itself was all in favor of the club. The player had no guarantee of making the team, and no guarantee of just what he might be paid for a given season if he failed. A one-year contract was taken for granted. Anything beyond that was unheard of for a rookie.

If Doug Orr knew little or nothing about all these circumstances and the pitfalls they represented for Bobby, at least he realized his ignorance in these matters. For that reason he decided the only answer for the youth was a lawyer who knew hockey and could speak for his client.

Through a mutual friend Doug met a young Toronto attorney who was perfect for the job. R. Alan Eagleson, a member of the legislative assembly of Ontario, was, in common with most of his compatriots, a wildly enthusiastic hockey fan.

It was impossible to be that and not have heard about Bobby Orr after Bobby's second year at Oshawa. The Canadian sports pages often reported his exploits on the ice and the fact that he was apparently headed for the Bruins.

When Bobby's father asked if he would help the family negotiate the contract to play for the Bruins, Eagleson was delighted to oblige.

That alliance between the Orr family and Alan Eagleson had a profound effect on professional hockey. For it was Eagleson who broke the barrier between NHL owners and players, and it was Eagleson who, more than any other

48

individual, was primarily responsible for the huge raises in salary later enjoyed by big-league hockey players everywhere.

Eagleson started with Bobby Orr. When he first tried to talk in Orr's name, the Bruins objected. They had never been in a situation like that—no one in the hockey hierarchy had. Their original intention was to move Bobby up to Boston, give him a nice, but not sensational salary, and from then on treat him as all the NHL owners had been treating their players.

This was exactly what Eagleson wanted to avoid. If the Orrs weren't sure of Bobby's worth, Alan Eagleson was certainly sure. He went to the Bruins—who finally arranged for the club attorney, Charles W. Mulcahy, Jr., to deal with him—and began a historic round of bargaining meetings.

The result was a spectacular contract for Bobby. Its exact figures were never announced and probably never will be known. The only feature revealed was the contract's duration: two years.

That alone was something new. Never in the history of the NHL had a rookie, regardless of his potential, been given more than a one-year contract. Seldom had any NHL players received anything but one-year contracts.

The lowest figure quoted for Bobby's first professional contract was $41,000—a shade over $20,000 a year. That would have been a record for hockey rookies, but it was probably too low. Far more probable is the rumor that Bobby was given a guarantee of $25,000 a year for two years, plus some fringe benefits, the nature of which were never disclosed.

Eagleson went on from there to help the entire league form a players' association, whereby all minimum salary contracts have been raised, as have awards for individual and team honors, and minimum payments for Stanley Cup play-offs.

What Eagleson did first for Bobby Orr, he has since done for at least 200 other professional hockey players. For some he didn't do as well, but he improved the incomes of all the men he represented.

Other lawyers and agents have gone into the field, but Eagleson was the first in hockey and Bobby Orr was his first client. Today the hockey moguls recognize him and others like him as the men with whom to deal in negotiating player contracts.

That is a far cry from the pre-Orr days when players negotiated their own contracts, very much to their disadvantage. They may not have realized it at the time, but they all needed an Alan Eagleson.

Thus, in a very substantial way Bobby Orr has contributed more heavily than any other professional hockey player to the well-being of his peers. And for that reason alone no one was ever jealous of him or resented the fact that his own income ranks today among the highest in professional sports.

Yet when Bobby first reported to the Bruins, he was just as nervous and scared as any other rookie.

After all, he was still only eighteen. There probably weren't half a dozen boys that age before him to make it in hockey's big time.

And there weren't any from whom so much was expected.

6 The First Year

The day Bobby Orr walked into the Bruins locker room for the first time a blanket was spread on the floor. The eighteen-year-old phenom, who described himself that day as "scared—real scared," had a feeling the blanket had something to do with him, but he wasn't sure exactly what until it was very briefly explained.

"Lay down on it," said a Bruin veteran about twice Bobby's age. "It's a magic blanket. We are going to make it rise."

Later, Orr admitted, "I half believed him. I fell into it like a real country hick."

If he hadn't fallen in, he would have been pushed in. The fifteen minutes that followed must still rank in his own mind as among the most uncomfortable of his life. One by one, each of the Bruins veterans shaved him from head to foot with a loose safety razor and no shaving cream.

By the time they got through scraping the wiggling blade, Orr's crew-cut head and most of the rest of his body was a mass of nicks and cuts. Not until everyone had had a turn did they let him up off the blanket. Since he had no choice, he took the initiation well. He couldn't have fought free if he had tried.

He thought at first it was standard procedure for any rookie to get scraped with a loose razor from head to foot by his teammates. Actually this was a special job for Bobby alone, and it had a practical purpose.

"We knew he'd be a marked man," one of the players later said. "No rookie has ever come into the NHL with more publicity. The whole league was waiting to give him the business. We felt it would be better for Bobby to get it from us first. After that, he would know that he would never be alone in a fight during a game."

This was—and still is—true. Few sports produce the intensity and team loyalty of professional hockey. Loyalty was always the biggest cause of free-for-all fights. When one man got into trouble, his whole team jumped in to help.

A strict NHL rule now has these fights pretty well under control. If anyone on the ice but the two original participants gets involved, he draws a heavy fine. If anyone jumps off the bench to join the battle, he draws a heavier fine.

Loyalty manifests itself in other ways. Teammates can always get even with an opponent for what may be a "cheap shot" at one of their own men. A so-called cheap shot is swinging on or otherwise belting an opponent when he can't see the blow coming or is in no position to fight back.

Fines or no fines, this will often start a free-for-all. A typical example can be seen at almost any professional hockey game. The minute a man is on the receiving end of an obvious cheap shot, he'll get help, even if it costs the men who help him money.

Since that first day when he was scraped with a razor while being held down on a blanket in the locker room, the Bruins players have had no more loyal ally than Bobby Orr. Whenever anyone was hurt by a cheap shot, Orr was one of the first men on the scene. A fearless and willing fighter himself, he was never afraid to defend a teammate.

One of the most striking situations involving Orr came in a preseason game of 1969 when Teddy Green suffered a depressed skull fracture in Ottawa after being hit over the head with the stick by Wayne Maki, then a St. Louis Blues rookie forward.

The moment Green went down, the whole Bruins bench came alive. Man after man jumped over the boards. Orr, who hadn't been on the ice when Green was hit, led the way.

The first man Bobby looked for was Maki, but the scared rookie had already retreated to the safety of his own bench. Then Orr skated over to Green who was being helped off the ice by Phil Esposito and a Bruins trainer, Dan Canney.

Orr said to Green, "Don't worry, Greenie. I'll get him."

Since Maki didn't play any more that night, Orr had no chance to "get" him then. Later Green, from his hospital bed in Ottawa, asked Bobby in particular not to "get" Maki.

Orr never did try, only because Green had asked him not to. There was a history of close association between Orr and Green that went back to Bobby's first year with the Bruins.

At that time Green was famous for being one of the toughest men in the NHL. He was continually getting into fights, mostly in defense of his teammates. When Orr joined the club, Green took the eighteen-year-old under his wing.

No one got into a fight with Orr without having to contend with Green, too. The veteran defenseman not only admired Bobby as the greatest hockey player he had ever seen, but loved him as a kid brother.

Orr never forgot Green's treatment at a time when he had needed help most. Great as he was on skates, he was still no more than a youngster, a fact nobody appreciated more than Green. A close friendship developed between the two that has lasted to this day.

The pressure on Orr was intensified by the fact that when he joined the Bruins in 1966, Green was one of only four or five players with the ability to stick long enough to share in the Bruins' later successes.

The new coach, Harry Sinden, was a brilliant young man who, although he had never played big-league hockey, had a big-league brain and knew how to handle big-league players.

The Bruins had hired Sinden to try to mold them into Stanley Cup champions. Smart as Sinden was, he couldn't hope to do much with what he had at the time. The Bruins were full of holes. Most of their men were too small. Except for Orr, Eddie Westfall, and Johnny Bucyk, they had no top players combining size with efficiency. Their best little man, John (Pie) McKenzie, a much-traveled veteran who joined the club in 1966, also helped them to Stanley Cup championships later.

They were hurting in the nets, since the only good goalie they had was Eddie Johnston. They needed a solid backup goalie and virtually an entire new set of lines. Their only real strength, other than Johnston at goal, was in defense where Green and Orr held steady.

The rest of the club that won a Stanley Cup title within four years was either playing elsewhere—to be obtained by the Bruins in trades—or in the minors or Junior A hockey.

The 1966–67 season was a disaster for the Bruins but a triumph for Orr. The sensational youngster seemed to be able to do everything. Although shooting from the left he could play either defense position. He was on both the power-play team and the penalty-killing team, an unusual situation in itself.

Orr's stamina was remarkable. He was on the ice at least fifty percent of each game. He could carry the puck, pass with the finesse of a veteran, and shoot with power.

Most satisfying of all to the Bruins brass, he wasn't afraid of defending himself. The toughest men in the league went after him and lived to regret it. For even at eighteen, Orr was far more powerful than he looked.

Just as his teammates expected, Bobby was a marked man wherever he went. With him the Bruins were a reasonably decent-looking big-league hockey team. Without him they were almost hopelessly ineffectual.

If one man could save them from oblivion, it was Bobby, but even he couldn't do the impossible. If nothing else, he proved that one man can't make a hockey team—he can only help brake its skid. Veterans like Green, Westfall, McKenzie, and Bucyk did what they could and so did Johnston in the nets, but nobody could stop the team from finishing in the cellar for the sixth time in seven years.

The Bruins were last in power-play scores, with 34 in 250 chances, and next to last in penalty killing. They were scored on 53 times in 240 shorthanded situations. From beginning to end they almost always had to play catch-up hockey because their opponents usually scored first.

But there was no doubt of what the hockey world thought of Orr. Some called him the best-looking rookie of all time. Others qualified it, calling him the "best-looking rookie since Beliveau."

Coach Billy Reay of the Black Hawks said of him, "He skates well, handles the puck well, shoots well, and passes well. What else do you want him to do? He's one kid who's lived up to his reputation."

"When he's on the ice," said King Clancy of Toronto, "the Bruins look like a hockey team. Without him they are nothing."

Emile Francis, coach and general manager of the Rangers, was no less lavish in his praise of Orr.

"I always said he'd be a better pro than a junior," Francis said. "I saw a lot of him as a junior. The kids would give him the puck and then they'd stand around and watch him. In the pros they get the puck to him and set themselves up for a return pass."

A few years later Francis commented, "I've looked at my score sheet after each Boston game, and there's Orr with seven or eight shots. One game against us he got twelve. He's a defenseman. He's not supposed to get that many shots. You'd think that since he's a defenseman he should spend more time defending. But we haven't caught him up the ice too often. Nobody ever does."

Win, lose, or draw, Orr pulled the fans back into the Boston Garden to watch the Bruins, not only after Christmas, but from the very start of the season. Their first two games in Boston were solid sellouts, and almost all their home games thereafter were sold out, too.

Orr was the attraction, not only in Boston, but everywhere the Bruins went. In Montreal, where the Canadiens are almost a religion, opening night was a sellout in 1966. More than 15,000 Montreal hockey fans went to the Forum that night to see Orr. And for Bobby the pressure was intense every time he faced a new team on the ice.

One night in Montreal Sinden sent him out on a power play. Using rookies on power plays was then almost unheard of in the NHL. It was too important an assignment, since it means trying to score in the two minutes the opponents are shorthanded.

Orr got the puck at the Canadiens' blue line, with Jim Roberts, Montreal's roughest penalty killer, coming right at him. Without losing his poise Bobby simply fended Roberts off, turned away from him, and backhanded the puck to Gilles Marotte.

"I always was a believer in Orr," said Red Fisher of the

Montreal *Star*. "And the way Bobby handled Roberts was the real clincher."

Orr had an assist in his first NHL game and a goal in his third. Both were milestones in his career, for they began a long string of goals and assists which eventually put him among the all-time NHL leaders.

Sinden, a former defenseman himself, was his greatest booster from the beginning.

"Orr may revolutionize the style for defensemen," said the rookie Bruins coach of his star. "He does things on offense nobody dared try before. He skates pretty deep into the attacking zone, yet he's always back in his regular position when we lose the puck."

Hap Emms, then in his final year as general manager of the Bruins, had spent most of his life working with youngsters in Junior A hockey. Normally very conservative, he was effusive in his praise for Orr.

"I don't think I've ever seen such a complete hockey player," he said. "Some players are great shooters, others fine passer and skaters, but Orr has everything. He also has something very special—God-given ability. He doesn't have to think. He makes the right move instinctively. All he needs is experience."

Bringing Sinden in as coach at the same time they brought Orr up as a player was a happy inspiration on the part of the Bruins. Sinden, only in his thirties at the time, could identify with the eighteen-year-old sensation. The two understood each other and got along well from the start.

Even at eighteen, Orr ran the games on the ice. He was always a pivotal performer, the man who started plays and often finished them. The older men were perfectly willing to accept Bobby as their leader on the ice because, as in any professional sport, the results are really all that count. For this reason alone, Orr's instinctive leadership was accepted by his teammates.

Some people thought there might be jealousy all over the league because of his salary. As a rookie, Orr's income compared with that of the top players in the game. It was generally accepted throughout the league that he was among its five highest paid men in his first year. The only higher paid players were Howe, Hull, Beliveau, and Frank Mahovlich.

But there was no jealousy on anybody's part. The youngster's teammates didn't begrudge him a cent of the hefty paycheck he was collecting. The opposition treated him as they treated any other rival player—they went after him because he was a dangerous, hard-shooting, daring hockey player. They didn't care if he made twenty-five thousand dollars or twenty-five cents.

Eagleson's formation of the NHL players' association began one day in December of 1966. While he and Orr were having dinner in a Montreal hotel, two of the Bruins asked if Eagleson would meet them in a room upstairs.

When the lawyer and his young client had finished eating they went up and found the entire Bruins team assembled there. They asked Eagleson to set the wheels in motion for a players' association. By the end of that season he had more than one hundred NHL players signed up. Eventually all but a few were in the fold.

During his first season in Boston Orr shared a small house with another Bruins rookie, Joe Watson, in the seaside suburb of Nahant. Watson was later a key defenseman with the Philadelphia Flyers, instrumental in their Stanley Cup championship in 1974. Because he was closest to Bobby in age, he was a natural roommate. The two got along well, just as Orr got along with all his roommates in the years he spent playing hockey.

After his first year in Boston Orr lived with the Bruins' assistant trainer, Frosty Foristall. The boys had two things in common beyond hockey—they were fairly close in age and neither was married. Orr didn't marry until 1973, when he was twenty-five.

Although later in his career Bobby was injured often, he stayed fairly free of physical ailments as a rookie. His worst mishap came in December, when he strained ligaments in one knee, which slowed him up for about a month but did not keep him out of action to any great extent.

Altogether he missed only 9 of the 70 games the Bruins played in the 1966–67 season. In the other 61 he made his presence so sharply felt that even though the Bruins finished last, their future as an NHL powerhouse was assured.

In midseason of his last year as general manager of the Bruins, Emms, asked how he would rate Orr among the other NHL players, replied, "I wouldn't trade him for the entire Maple Leaf team."

Since that was one of the years the Leafs won the Stanley Cup, this was perhaps as great a tribute as anyone had given Orr all season.

He ended it in a blaze of glory. His 13 goals led the league's defensemen. Gordie Howe, an all-time Red Wing superstar and a forward, had had only 7 goals his rookie year.

Orr, close to perfect as he might have been, was only human, which he proved by the occasional mistakes he made as a rookie. Once, against the Canadiens in Boston, he let John Ferguson slip around him and score.

In a game against Detroit Orr was on the ice for 5 Red Wings goals and was directly responsible for the first 3. That was probably his worst game of the season, but the Bruins fans forgave him.

"They would have forgiven him if he had been on the

ice for fifteen goals," Sinden said. "He could have slipped five of them into his own net and they would have forgiven him. The kid is so good most of the time that everyone forgives his mistakes. He doesn't make enough to worry about anyhow."

He made a bad mistake once against the Rangers while still a whiffle-haired rookie. One night he took a small half-turn with the puck in his own zone when Vic Hadfield, the New York left wing, yelled, "Drop it, Bobby. Drop it."

Thinking it was one of his own teammates, Orr dropped it back, and Hadfield picked it up and scored.

If nothing else, that taught Bobby a very important hockey lesson—to learn to recognize the voices of his own teammates, and those of everyone else in the NHL as well.

Hadfield's trick, one of the oldest in hockey, may have been repeated several times, but Orr never fell for it again.

Nobody knew Bobby's own mistakes and how to correct them better than Bobby himself. Early in his rookie season Sinden kept after him to get his shots down. He was too high when going for a goal.

"Maybe you ought to change the lie of your stick or use a different blade," Sinden suggested.

"That's not it at all," Orr said. "I'm not following through low enough. I'll work on it."

Later, when Sinden saw that Bobby *was* getting off lower shots without either changing the lie of his stick or using a different blade, the Bruins coach said, "The kid knew all about it and his coach didn't. In those areas where he's weak he knows the trouble better than anyone."

Perhaps Jean Beliveau of the Canadiens, another of hockey's superstars at the time Orr first came up to the Bruins, expressed Bobby's situation better than anyone.

"Nobody is a perfect hockey player," Beliveau said. "The important thing is to correct your mistakes. Orr, he does that. Sometimes it seems he is off balance and you start to move by him, and then he is there. He is always there. He blocks the shots. He can skate. He can shoot. Is there anything more?"

The rest of the National Hockey League players and brass obviously didn't think so, nor did the hockey writers.

In midseason he was the only rookie on the second All-Star team. And in the voting of the Calder Trophy for the outstanding rookie of the year, he won the award by a huge margin.

And that was only the beginning.

For Bobby Orr, the instant superstar, obviously had a long and illustrious hockey career ahead of him.

7 A Brand-New Hockey Team

The National Hockey League, after dragging its feet for years, suddenly doubled in size in 1967. While the original league of six teams remained intact as the so-called East Division, a West Division was set up of six entirely new teams.

The West Division included St. Louis, Minnesota, Philadelphia, Pittsburgh, Los Angeles, and Oakland, the latter designated as the California Seals. The clubs were stocked by players from established teams in an expansion draft similar to those in other professional sports.

Since each of the original teams protected its best men, the expansion clubs got a collection of rejects, faded veterans, and untried youngsters. It was partly for this reason that the 1970 Bruins had no problem sweeping the finals of the Stanley Cup play-offs. They were a sound team of great players, while the St. Louis Blues, the West finalists, were still building after only three years.

Expansion meant, if nothing else, better individual offensive records for the men on the original teams. However, it did not change the competition within the East Division. It was just as hard for the Bruins, for example, to beat the Canadiens as it ever had been, and just as hard for Bobby Orr to outplay the opposition when a rival East team was facing the Bruins.

It was that season—the 1967–68 campaign—that found the Bruins, for the first time in nearly a decade, strong contenders in the race for the play-offs. That year, the team was loaded with new men of class and ability, the true nucleus of the great Bruins teams that immediately followed.

Hap Emms was relieved as general manager by Milt Schmidt, and the effect of the move was not only a new look, but a new attitude. Schmidt, one of the greatest centers who ever lived, had been the star of the legendary Bruins' Kraut Line, consisting of himself, Woody Dumart and Bobby Bauer. The three spearheaded the Bruins to two Stanley Cups in the three seasons between 1938 and 1941.

Emms, haughty and unapproachable and more a teacher than a general manager, rarely, if ever, walked into the Bruins locker room. His many years in Junior A hockey had developed in him a separation from the players. His Junior A boys saw him as the teacher he was, and he couldn't help acting the role in Boston.

The result was a coolness toward him on the part of the Bruins players, which didn't help build morale within the organization, nor did it build much loyalty between the players and the front office. Emms's failure to identify with the pros was the principal reason for this lack of *esprit de corps*.

Sinden helped somewhat to counteract it, but the coach couldn't do it alone. A link was needed between the locker room and the executive department.

Schmidt provided that link. Instead of ignoring the players, as Emms had, he visited them often, sometimes spending as much time around the locker room as in his office. At heart a player, he was a players' general manager.

The players, in turn not only respected him for his own magnificent record as a player, but liked him personally. Schmidt, an easygoing, friendly man, was, as a matter of fact, just about everything Emms hadn't been. He listened to individual problems, did what he could to help, and always kept open the lines of communication between players and front office.

At the same time he did nothing to interfere with Sinden's job as coach. Schmidt was there to help, not hinder. Normally a general manager is not too welcome by the coach in a locker room. Sinden, however, liked Schmidt as much as the players did. The two worked together very well.

Schmidt was no stranger to the locker room even after he retired as a player. In all the years since, he had never left the Boston organization. Among other things, he had served as coach on two different occasions, so he knew the problems of the job as well as Sinden did.

Schmidt could particularly identify with Bobby Orr. As with other Bruins executives who had first seen Orr play as a twelve-year-old, Schmidt had a sort of proprietary interest in Bobby. But he also had closer ties to Orr than that.

Like Orr, Schmidt had broken into the NHL at the age of eighteen. Old-timers who compared him with Orr made him feel good, but he refused to accept the similarity. To Schmidt, as to so many others, Orr was the greatest all-around hockey player the game had ever seen.

But Schmidt had enough pride in his own record to recognize that they were close in many respects, and had had similar problems breaking into the league.

Schmidt had been a tall, reedy kid. Orr, only a bit shorter, was just as reedy. Like Orr, Schmidt had come from a much smaller community than Boston, although his home, Kitchener, Ontario, was considerably larger than Parry Sound.

Actually Schmidt had help adjusting to the big city, because he hadn't had to face it alone, as Orr did. Schmidt had come to Boston with Dumart, a lifelong friend with whom he had grown up in Kitchener. And a year later Bauer, another Kitchener boy, joined them.

There was, of course, a technical difference between Schmidt and Orr on the ice because Schmidt had been a center and Orr a defenseman. This had little to do with the similarities between them, however. Both were magnificent skaters, fierce competitors, and great shooters and passers.

Schmidt was the only member of the line he centered to be elected to hockey's Hall of Fame in Toronto. He played for the Bruins sixteen years and retired only because he had taken such a physical beating during his career that he could no longer move at top speed.

Many Orr-watchers feel that Bobby's career will—as it has in so many ways already—parallel Schmidt's career more than Eddie Shore's. All that Orr and Shore really had in common was that both were defensemen who could carry the puck down the ice and shoot.

Although not a defenseman, Schmidt was generally considered a better all-around hockey player than Shore, who is also in hockey's Hall of Fame. Orr holds the same distinction as Schmidt—he was certainly a better all-around player than Shore.

Schmidt deems Orr a better all-around player than he himself had been. If this is true, the difference was little more than a shade. However, there is little doubt that, like Schmidt, Orr will be stopped by injuries before he is stopped by age.

If Schmidt had not made the Hall of Fame as a player, he might have made it as an executive for the job he did building the Bruins from a cellar team to a Stanley Cup winner in three years. Once Orr joined the club in 1966, most of the rest of the future champions followed a year later, thanks to Schmidt's efforts.

When Schmidt became the general manager, the Bruins had, among others, Bucyk, Westfall, and McKenzie as forwards, Orr and Green as defensemen, and Johnston in the nets. These men formed the core of the Stanley Cup championship team.

But six top men don't make an NHL hockey team. The Bruins needed more defensemen and another goalie. Since all the big forwards were wings, the club also had to find three first-class centers. Schmidt dug up all three in time for the 1967–68 campaign, Orr's second in the league.

One, Phil Esposito, came in one of the most astounding trades ever made. Another, Derek Sanderson, was twenty-one years old, and his experience up to then had been mainly in Junior A hockey at Niagara Falls. The third, Fred Stanfield, was part of the deal that brought Esposito to the Bruins.

That trade was completed by Schmidt in May of 1967, right after he became the club's general manager. But he had spent weeks setting it up when he was assistant general manager, bargaining back and forth with Tommy Ivan, the Chicago Black Hawks general manager.

Ivan, highly respected as an executive, did not make many mistakes while in the Chicago front office, but in his trade with the Bruins, he was badly outsmarted by Schmidt.

Although new to the job of general manager, Schmidt knew exactly what was wrong with the Bruins. As a squad they were too small. Remembering that the Bruins' Stanley Cup teams on which he played himself were made up mostly of big, rugged men, he determined to build the new Bruins into the same type of team.

Esposito, six feet one and two hundred ten pounds, had

the ideal build from Schmidt's standpoint. He could shoot, and he was big enough to fight off defenders trying to get him out of the slot. This is the area directly in front of the nets, the place where a center belongs when the team is deep in opposition territory.

The Hawks were willing to trade Esposito because they didn't think he could score in play-off competition. Actually up to then he hadn't done well in play-offs. In four years he had twice been held scoreless, once to 1 goal and once to 3.

Stanfield, five ten and one hundred eighty-five pounds, had not yet proved himself as a big-league hockey player. He had spent the previous two years in the minors, and the Hawks simply gave up on him. Schmidt disagreed with them. In his judgment Stanfield was ready for the NHL, and if Chicago were willing to give him up, Schmidt was willing to take him.

The third man the Hawks were willing to give up was Ken Hodge, whom they considered a lazy hockey player. In the two seasons this six-foot-two, two hundred sixteen-pound right wing had been at Chicago, he had scored a total of only 16 goals.

Schmidt thought Hodge could do much better than that. Schmidt knew him well because he had once had him at a hockey school he had run a few years earlier in Canada. Hodge had looked promising then, and Schmidt was sure he could help the Bruins.

And Hodge was big—the biggest man the Bruins got in that trade. Like Esposito, he was rugged enough to fight off anyone.

In return for those three men the Bruins gave the Black Hawks Gilles Marotte, Pit Martin, and Jack Norris. Marotte was a five-foot-nine defensemen and Martin a five-eight center. Norris was a minor-league goalie.

While in retrospect the trade seemed a steal for the Bruins, at the time some thought the Hawks had gotten the best of it. Martin was an outstanding center, who made up in speed and guts what he lacked in height. Marotte was a good defenseman. Norris actually was a throw-in because the Hawks needed a goalie for one of their minor-league clubs.

But as it turned out, Esposito alone would have been worth the deal to the Bruins. Six years later he was a superstar who had smashed all league scoring records not once but several times, and had the highest goal average per year in NHL history.

If he had weaknesses in play-off competition at Chicago, he certainly didn't show them in Boston. He was as good in play-offs as in the regular season after he joined the Bruins.

And he was the man who saved Team Canada from embarrassment and frustration in the 1972 series against the Russians. If it had not been for Esposito's ability to score, the Canadians would have lost that series. As it was, they barely won it, 4 games to 3, with one game ending in a tie.

While neither Stanfield nor Hodge could hope to match Esposito, both more than lived up to Schmidt's expectations. Hodge was anything but a lazy hockey player for the Bruins. He scored 25 or more goals in 4 of his first 5 seasons at Boston and tipped 40 in 2 of those.

Stanfield didn't fail to score 20 goals in any of his first 5 seasons, while centering one of the Bruins' regular lines.

By the end of the 1973 season, although Stanfield was traded to Minnesota, Esposito and Hodge were still important Bruins players.

On the other hand, the only man Schmidt sent to Chicago in the trade who survived as long with the Hawks was Martin. Marotte was traded to the Los Angeles Kings, and Norris never played a full season in the NFL.

Several of the Bruins of 1967–68 were rookies brought up by Schmidt, whom Emms hadn't thought were ready. Sanderson was the prize package, for this youngster from Niagara was such a stickout that he won the Calder Trophy for being the league's outstanding rookie. Since Orr had won it the previous season, it gave the Bruins the NHL's top rookies two years in a row.

Schmidt also brought up two defensemen and an outstanding goalie. Don Awrey, from Hershey, and Dallas Smith, from Oklahoma City, strengthened the defense. The two, both left defensemen, made it possible to split up Orr and Green, who had been working together.

But although Bobby could and did play left defense, he was more comfortable on the right side, where he could team up with Smith. And Green, who had to play right defense, found a most effective partner in Awrey.

Another of Schmidt's major decisions was promoting Gerry Cheevers from Oklahoma City to the Bruins. Cheevers, a rapidly improving goalie, had already twice been bounced up and down between Boston and Oklahoma City while others were getting the chance to back up Ed Johnston.

As Schmidt had expected, Cheevers developed into a star who gave the Bruins additional strength in a spot where they had badly needed help.

After one season with very little help from his mates Bobby Orr was now in a position to help the Bruins move up in the standings. He could certainly help a good team much more than a poor one. By surrounding him with a good team Schmidt had done his part.

Now it was up to Bobby to do his.

8 Injuries—Injuries—Injuries

The summer of 1967 was a nightmare for shy, young Bobby Orr. His magnificent rookie season with the Bruins had made him a national celebrity in his native Canada. He was not only invited, but begged, cajoled and ordered to appear at sports functions almost everywhere they were held.

It was impossible for him to accept everything. As it was, he made the mistake of trying to satisfy more people and groups than anyone would reasonably be expected to.

He never disappointed anyone once he promised to be somewhere. But he made so many commitments that between the end of his rookie hockey season and the middle of July, he didn't spend a single weekend with his family in Parry Sound.

To some young bachelors this sort of life would have been a pleasure. To Orr it was just an annoyance. He dearly loved all his immediate family, his parents and brothers and sisters, and enjoyed being with them.

In July he rather plaintively said, "I like being with people, but I wouldn't want to go through that again."

And from then on, he never did. No matter how much

he found himself in demand, he always left a certain number of weekends free to be in Parry Sound.

During the summer, in a charity exhibition hockey game in Winnipeg, he suffered a slight ligament tear in his right knee. He had played in violation of his contract with the Bruins, which specifically barred participation in such games.

It wasn't a bad injury, but the Bruins were upset. Yet with typical understanding, Milt Schmidt remarked, "I'd probably have done the same thing myself at his age."

Despite the injury, which was slow in healing, Bobby couldn't wait for preseason practice at London, Ontario. Although he wasn't ready to play, he reported on opening day—"to be with the guys," as he put it.

He wasn't able to skate, but he worked hard with weights and on a stationary bicycle to strengthen the knee. Within a few days he put on skates and tried to work out, but the going was too tough and Sinden made him quit.

"I had to chase him off the ice," the young Bruins coach said. "If I hadn't, he might have aggravated the injury."

But Bobby wouldn't quit for long. Besides being a great skater when physically sound, he loved it and resented not being able to go at top speed. He got such a thrill out of feeling the blades under his feet that he wouldn't wear stockings.

"My bare feet in skating shoes give me a feeling of power on the ice," he explained, when asked about his somewhat unusual habit.

No one knows how many youngsters are growing up skating without stockings just because Orr does. But there is no question that many budding skaters are copying him in that respect, as they try to do in so many others.

Hockey purists advise young skaters not to try to copy Orr in anything, because he broke too many conventional rules. For one thing, he often carried the puck out by crossing in front of his own net, a dangerous move by a defenseman because if he loses the puck in the slot his goalie may be at the mercy of the opponent who steals it.

And the very thing that helped make Orr great was a violation of hockey convention. Defensemen are not supposed to venture too far down the ice, for fear they can't get back if the other team gets the puck and attacks.

Yet nobody could criticize Orr for these and other ways in which he defied hockey tradition and what is generally accepted as sound hockey practice because his plays succeeded despite the violations.

He had such fine control that he rarely lost the puck. And he was so fast that even when an opposing wing got a head start on him, Orr could win a race back to his own zone to handle his defensive duties.

Bobby finally got medical clearance to start skating again prior to the opening of the 1967–68 season about two weeks after practice began at London. Three days later he suffered a groin pull and was ordered to rest in bed for four days.

It was all a prelude of things to come, for this was to be a year of injuries, a long succession of injuries that hampered Orr's activities all season.

Bobby couldn't understand it.

"I've been playing hockey all my life," he said one day. "I never used to get hurt this much. Even last year, when the whole league was gunning for me, I could play most of the time. I can't figure this out."

When he got back onto skates, he war far behind the rest of the league. It took him weeks to regain his timing and speed.

In the meantime the Orr-less Bruins got off to a poor start, prompting Sinden to remark, "Orr, at nineteen, is the guy who can pull this team together. We miss him every day he's on the shelf."

On one of the nights Bobby was out of action, the Maple Leafs beat them, 4–2, in Boston.

"Maybe the Bruins missed Orr," said Punch Imlach, the Leafs' coach, after the game. "But I didn't."

On the night Bobby returned to NHL competition, Brian Conacher of the Leafs broke Orr's nose, starting a wild brawl in which Bobby broke a thumb throwing punches.

The next morning he skated in practice with the club and was back in action in time to help win the next Bruins game.

He slugged and fought and skated and scored his way through the month that followed, leading the Bruins in a drive that landed them in first place by the end of November. In the meantime Bobby continued to get smashed by opponents, piling up one injury after another.

By December he had collected, besides the summer-game knee injury and preseason groin injury, a muscle strain in his back, two broken noses, two broken thumbs and two deep cuts requiring no fewer than six stitches each.

But except for a game here and there he kept on going, dishing out as much punishment as he gave and rarely missing his turns on the ice. This included extra duty on power plays and penalty-killing teams.

With all the new talent the Bruins could present very respectable special units. Sinden often used all three of his centers, Esposito, Stanfield, and Sanderson, on the power play team, along with Orr and either Hodge or Bucyk.

The penalty-killing unit was usually Bobby, Stanfield, and Pie McKenzie or Bucyk, Cashman, and Esposito. While others were often shifted around, Bobby was almost always on the ice when the chips were down.

It was an odd sensation when the Minnesota North Stars arrived in Boston for the first game of the year between the two clubs. Minnesota's general manager was Wren Blair, Bobby's former Junior A mentor at Oshawa.

The two were delighted to see each other but, although still fast friends, they were now professional rivals. Blair expressed his own reaction by saying, "It's a funny feeling. I have never been in a hockey game where Bobby has played against me. After having him for four years at Oshawa, I know what he can do to you."

"The guy was always so great to me and did so much for me I hate to hurt him," Orr said. "But once out there on the ice, my job is to beat the opponent, no matter who he is."

Actually the Bruins had little trouble with the new expansion team, with Bobby as usual playing a big part in their victory. He and Blair often met for dinner when the teams played each other after that, but when in uniform, Bobby thought of nothing but victory.

It was little different from the situations that arose when the Esposito brothers faced each other, as they often did after Phil was traded to Boston.

His brother, Tony, who had joined the Black Hawks and remained in Chicago after Phil was traded, was one of the best goalies in hockey. Wherever the Bruins and the Hawks met, the brothers, who were very close, spent all their spare time together.

But on the ice they were enemies. With reference to the two Espositos, an observer once remarked, "In this league, ice is thicker than blood once the game starts."

In mid-December at Toronto Bobby collided with Frank Mahovlich, but even that didn't stop him, at least that night. He was hurt in the first period, but played the whole game.

That was the Bruins' eighth straight victory, and Bobby had played a key part in all eight. The injury forced him to the sidelines, where he watched the expansion Los An-

75

geles Kings beat the Bruins in Boston in the first game he missed after the injury.

He was out only seventeen days, missing but seven games. The Bruins didn't lose all seven, but they were in trouble.

After the Canadiens beat them one night, their coach, Toe Blake, told Boston writers, "Trouble is, you've lost your general. He makes all the difference, just as every great player does. Bobby rallies other players around him, and he takes charge. He solves the big problems whether they're offensive or defensive."

Back the day after Christmas Orr did pull the team together, and they got back on the right track. With all his injuries Bobby had played in 25 of the previous 32 games.

But he suffered an injury to his right shoulder in Philadelphia soon after New Year's, and that put him back on the shelf for several days.

He was back in action in time for the All-Star game against the Leafs at Toronto on January 16, at nineteen the youngest man ever to play in the game.

Besides the honor of playing, Bobby was all over the ice, keeping the All-Stars in the game, which the Leafs won, 4–3. With a minute left, Bobby just missed scoring the tying goal on a power play. He later was voted the outstanding player in the game.

But what few knew was that Bobby played most of it with a broken collarbone. He fractured it when Pete Stemkowski of the Leafs checked him heavily into the boards.

Two spectators who knew almost immediately that Orr was hurt were Milt Schmidt and Harry Sinden. However, since they also knew that Bobby was enjoying the game and wouldn't come out unless seriously injured, they didn't try to interfere.

"I've never seen him when he isn't trying to live up to his reputation," Sinden said. "What this means is that he won't tell anyone when he's hurt. Unless you catch him off guard or several bones are broken, you never really know. All he ever says when you ask him is, 'I'm all right. I'm all right.' And when Stemkowski hit him, he just kept on going because he felt he had to live up to the honor of being an All-Star."

But Schmidt wasn't quite so calm about Orr staying in the game, especially in its late stages. In the last few minutes the Bruins' general manager, with visions of his great star going back on the sick list, yelled to All-Star Coach Toe Blake to send him to the locker room.

Blake didn't hear Schmidt, and instead of the locker room, Orr went back on the ice for the last couple of minutes.

Actually Blake never did know that Orr was hurt until the game was over. Even if he had suspected it, he probably wouldn't have believed it from the way Bobby was playing.

Only in the locker room did Orr himself realize it might be serious.

"I hardly noticed it while I was playing," he said. "But later in the night I had trouble lifting my arm."

The injury kept him out of 5 games. Soon after he returned, he hurt his left knee in a game against the St. Louis Blues. That was on February 7.

Four nights later, in a game at Detroit's Olympia Stadium, even Bobby had to admit he was in real trouble when his left knee locked the first time he set his foot on the ice. The game hadn't even started when Orr was ordered back to Boston for a thorough physical exam.

He returned the next day, showing a touch of temper for one of the few times in his career. Some reporters had been writing about his "brittleness," making it evident they thought the great Bobby Orr was so injury-prone he could never really help the team win a Stanley Cup title.

While he had suffered an enormous number of injuries and while his knees were apparently especially susceptible, there was no reason to predict disaster for a nineteen-year-old boy. Bad knees have shelved a lot of athletes who later came back to star. Many great ones have suffered more than their share of injuries, then returned to lead a team to glory.

Bobby justifiably resented the implication that he was too brittle, too prone to injury.

When his plane arrived at Boston's Logan Airport, it was met by hundreds of fans and half a dozen newsmen. For the first time he walked through the crowds without raising his head, while trying to fend off inquiring reporters asking about his knee.

"I don't know," he kept repeating. "I just don't know. Please—I don't want to talk about it."

When Dr. Ronald Adams, the team physician, announced that the removal of a cartilage in his left knee was "completely successful," Bruins followers were grateful that Bobby would be back in good shape the next season.

But the Bruins were battling for second place in the East Division and Orr was badly needed to keep them in the race. While everyone else, including Bobby himself, thought he was through for the year, the club brass seriously considered trying to get him back on the ice before the season's end.

The operation had taken place around mid-February. Knee operations almost always take three or four months to heal. Hardly a month had gone by when the Bruins announced Orr was ready to work out and might play before the season ended.

Many hockey players and sports experts shook their heads. Some openly called it dangerous exploitation of a great young talent—something that might finish him for good. Doctors in particular insisted the Bruins were rushing

78

Orr back much too soon, that they had allowed nowhere nearly enough time for his recovery.

But Orr did work out and a week before the regular season ended he was given a medical okay to face the Red Wings in Detroit.

As usual he wanted to play, but he couldn't conceal some concern.

"I just don't know how I'll feel," he said. "I'm like a guy going into his first game."

He was nervous, under tremendous pressure and obviously worried about getting hurt. He made it through the first period, but in the second got into an argument with Bill Friday, the referee.

When it appeared to Friday that Orr put his hand to his neck in a classic "choke-up" sign, the referee pinned a ten-minute misconduct penalty on him.

When Bobby went into the penalty box, he slammed the door so hard the protective glass grazed Friday's nose.

"That's another ten minutes for *you*," Friday yelled. "You're out of the game."

That released enough tension so that Bobby suddenly broke into a grin.

"Bill," he said, "I didn't know you were there. If I did, I'd have slammed the door harder."

With Orr out, the Bruins lost a 5–3 decision, but in his condition they probably would have lost anyhow. He showed that he wasn't himself in the next game, too, when the Bruins lost their last chance for second place by dropping a 5–4 decision to the Rangers in Boston.

The Bruins finished third and in the play-offs without Orr for nearly half the season. Of the 74 games they played, Bobby was in only 46. Even so, he scored 11 goals, only 2 fewer than in his rookie season, and had 20 assists, which was but 8 short of his first-year total.

Although he had no business on the ice, Orr took part in the play-offs. With his knee still bothering him, his whole performance suffered. He played strictly conventional defense, rarely going off on one of his patented sorties up the ice.

His premature return did no permanent damage, but his presence in the lineup failed to help the Bruins. They needed a sound Bobby Orr, not a one-legged one. He couldn't skate with his usual dash, nor could he shoot as well.

The club did poorly. After eight straight years out of the play-offs, the appearance they finally made was mediocre. They dropped all 4 of the quarter-final games to the Montreal Canadiens.

Orr's figures reflected his condition. He failed to get a goal and collected only 2 assists in the 4 games. He was so obviously not himself that Sinden kept him on the bench much of the time.

It was an unhappy ending to what gave promise of being a great season. And when it was over, nobody, least of all Bobby himself, had any idea where he was going.

9 Hockey's Money Tree

The nightmare of the 1967–68 season ended, but Bobby Orr's troubles didn't. As soon as the play-offs were finished, he headed home to Parry Sound, determined to rest up, enjoy life in the atmosphere he loved and gradually work his way back into good physical shape.

But, to his dismay, his knee began bothering him almost the day he arrived home. It took him several weeks to believe there was anything wrong. After the operation and the clean bill of health from the doctors, he was sure his knee would be the last of his worries.

By May it was obvious he had to do something. That time he went to Dr. John Palmer in Toronto, who confirmed the knee problem was serious. There was a cartilage chip, which may or may not have developed during his abortive attempt to come back.

No one will ever know if Orr would have had more trouble in his left knee even if he had rested instead of trying to play. But the Bruins certainly didn't cover themselves with glory in their handling of him.

Badly as they needed him, both he and they might have

been better off had he rested instead of trying to do the impossible. Perhaps the trouble would have come even if he had rested. But there was no question that the few games he tried to play did the knee no good.

His second knee operation in less than five months was performed in June of 1968. Then, after the surgery was pronounced successful, Bobby went back to Parry Sound with more hope than real optimism. He was worried.

Was he doomed to oblivion—through at the tender age of twenty? Would he ever make it back, and, if healed, how good would he be?

No one knew the possibilities better than Orr. Knee injuries are always tricky. Most athletes take a year or more to recover completely—when they recover at all.

The major factor in Bobby's favor was his youth. The older the athlete, the more serious any injury, and the more serious the injury, the longer the recovery. Young as he was, there was a good chance Bobby might come back quickly.

The operation had been a success. There was no pressure to get back into action in a hurry. The Bruins weren't due to meet for pregame practice until the following September. That was three months away. For a twenty-year-old it would be possible to start the new season and probable that he could be as good as ever within a month.

He hobbled around Parry Sound on crutches for several weeks. In accordance with doctor's orders he did prescribed exercises, enjoyed life as much as he could, and, as time went on, became more and more optimistic.

The knee was healing. There was no doubt about that. Back in Toronto for examinations, he was told to discard the crutches.

One beautiful summer day Bobby and a host of friends went to a secluded section of the Bay and held a crutch-burning party. While hundreds cheered, the crutches went up in smoke in a big clump of bushes.

Not until they were burned to a crisp did the party end. Bobby's face was split in an ear-to-ear grin. He could walk easily without crutches, and it wouldn't be long before he would be skating again.

If Bobby had any doubts about his future, the men in whose hands much of it lay certainly didn't. Alan Eagleson, the attorney who had negotiated his first contract with the Bruins, went back into action before Bobby was off crutches. As Orr's representative, he sat down with Bruins officials to work out a new contract.

The first one in many ways had been a record contract for a rookie. Eagleson was determined to make Bobby's second contract the most lucrative in the history of the National Hockey League.

The game was still lagging behind other major professional sports—baseball, football, and basketball—in player salaries. Hockey had been the lowest paying sport for so long that its prestige and standing had suffered.

True, thanks to Bobby's first contract, the league's top stars had been able to claim more than they had ever been paid before. Gordie Howe, who had been in the NHL before Bobby was born, Bobby Hull, who wasn't much younger than Howe, Jean Beliveau, Frank Mahovlich, and Stan Mikita were in higher income brackets because of Bobby.

Players with less fame or ability could also command more money, partly because of Orr and partly because big television money was finally available since the expansion. The whole league had been upgraded, and the blond kid from Parry Sound had led the way.

But unlike other sports, hockey still had no $100,000-a-year players by the time the 1967–68 season ended. Baseball had half a dozen with the number increasing all the time. Football's top-paid athletes, especially quarterbacks, were in or near six figures. Basketball had several men with multiple-year contracts in the same salary bracket.

Under the circumstances Eagleston felt it was time for hockey to catch up, and the man to do it should be Bobby Orr.

Orr had lived up to all the promise he had showed before he reached the NHL. More than lived up to it, in fact. Already, after only two seasons, one of which was halved by injuries, he was being hailed as the greatest player in the game's history.

Everyone in the Bruins' organization respected him. The coach built the team around him. The general manager obtained the men for the coach to build with. The owners told the world that they were honored to have Bobby in their organization.

The writers who covered the Bruins respected him both as a player and as a man.

He was what is known in the writing trade as an "easy interview." He was courteous and cooperative, answered most questions readily and without pulling punches, and rarely clammed up on a writer. He still called strangers approaching him "sir" or "mister" or "ma'am."

When he made appointments, he kept them. He almost never showed annoyance or irritation. Even after the heat of a hard game he talked readily to those whose job it was to get quotes from him.

In Boston he was every fan's idol: a superb hockey player, and a charming young man.

His relationship with his teammates was unusually warm. They almost all considered him one of their closest friends.

Many superstars' closest friends were people not involved in sports.

84

Very few were like Orr. Bobby, of course, did have friends outside hockey or not with the Bruins, but his warmth and friendliness always included his teammates. Bobby liked people, and the people he saw constantly during the hockey season were his teammates. The mutual warmth between them and Bobby was genuine and natural.

The dickering between Eagleson and the Bruins brass continued while Orr was convalescing from his second knee operation. The Bruins were not hard to deal with.

"The Bruins realize what a fabulous property Bobby is and are willing to pay what he's worth," Eagleson was quoted as saying. "He has produced beyond our expectations, beyond theirs, beyond anyone's. Boston is a .500 club without Bobby and around .700 when he's in the lineup."

That was the difference between breaking even in wins and losses during the season and getting into the play-offs or winning the Prince of Wales Cup, emblematic of the East Division championship.

In practical terms it was the difference between selling out the Boston Garden for every game and having empty seats.

People who can not beg, borrow, or steal a ticket to a Bruins game in Boston during Orr's years find it hard to believe that the same tickets had sometimes gone begging before Bobby joined the club. It had become so difficult to get anything but gallery rush seats that even the owners had trouble digging up tickets for friends and associates.

All of which were arguments in Boby's favor at contract time. Eagleson could have used these arguments. Perhaps he didn't need to.

While negotiations were going on, someone asked a Bruins official if the club had doubts about his physical condition.

"Not really," was the reply. "Bobby's young and will

come back fast. Why, the greatest two previous stars on our club, Eddie Shore and Milt Schmidt, were always getting hurt. In the sixteen years he played for us I doubt if Schmidt had a single full season."

Another said, "Orr goes at full speed every minute he's on the ice. This is a rugged business. No human being could play it the way Bobby does without getting hurt. Injuries are part of the game."

When the final terms of the contract were hammered out by Eagleson and Charles W. Mulcahy, Jr., the Bruins' general counsel, they emerged with what was indeed a record contract. As some observers noted, it was so lush that it "put hockey right into the big time."

For the three years beginning with the 1968–69 season Bobby was to get an estimated $400,000, or more than $125,000 a season. There were also several fringe benefits.

Orr was guaranteed a job in the Boston organization for the next twenty-five years. He was given a substantial life-insurance policy, payable to his family. He was to receive a $25,000 bonus if the Bruins won the Stanley Cup.

All this was rumor and rumor only. The Bruins and Orr refused to discuss the contract, but most of its reported terms were probably fairly accurate. Whatever the situation, it certainly upgraded hockey from the standpoint of salaries and had tremendous impact on the NHL.

When Gordie Howe went to the Red Wing owners with a clipping reporting Orr's new contract, they tore up his old pact and gave him a new one with a big increase. When Bobby Hull heard about Orr's paycheck, he threatened to retire in 1968 unless the Hawks paid him in six figures. They agreed.

Others around the league demanded—and got—more money than they had ever dreamed of. Not only superstars, but everybody benefited from Bobby's new contract.

In all seriousness Bobby said, "I hope I can put money in everybody's pocket. For that matter, I hope everyone can get twice as much as I'm getting."

Other Bruins players were among those to benefit. A great team was in the making and Bobby wasn't its only star. Phil Esposito, Johnny Bucyk, Teddy Green, Eddie Johnston, Derek Sanderson, Fred Stanfield, Ken Hodge, Pie McKenzie, Gerry Cheevers, Dallas Smith, and Don Awrey were all headed for new financial heights—thanks to Orr and his astute attorney.

Even before he reported for preseason training in London, Ontario, Bobby was asked if he felt players on other clubs would go after him harder because of the size of his paycheck.

"I don't think so," Bobby said. "They didn't exactly treat me with kid gloves in my first two seasons, you know. I expect to get dumped on occasion and I expect I'll knock a few guys down, too. Putting it simply, if they come looking for me, they know where to find me."

Later, because his salary was brought to his attention almost everywhere he went, he began to get annoyed.

"So much baloney has been written about it," he said one day. "Sometimes it bothers me a little. I wouldn't go up to another fellow and ask him what he makes, and I think I'm entitled to the same treatment."

Then, with typical Orr courtesy, he added, "Not that I don't understand. Writers have a job to get stories and fans are interested in what athletes make. I am myself when I read about guys in other sports."

Even when annoyed about it, Bobby accepted with grins the needling his teammates sometimes gave him. One day a large package was delivered to him in the Bruins locker room.

"What's that?" somebody yelled. "Your money for the week?"

The only type of heckling that really infuriated him was when it came from disgruntled fans.

"I know the fans pay my salary," he once said. "And I try to do my best to be nice to them. Most of them have been just super to me and I appreciate it. I sign as many autographs as I can and acknowledge individual good wishes whenever I see people at the rink or anywhere else.

"But if I have a real bad game," he said, "I find it's better to get out as fast as I can. You never know when some wise guy will yell something that really gets you mad. You want to hit him, but you can't—that just makes a bad situation worse. So I don't pay attention."

His high salary also brought some unwelcome correspondence from strangers. Several people demanded to know why a player who made mistakes—as they all do, from time to time, even Bobby—had a right to collect the kind of money Orr was earning. He ignored most of the unfair criticism, although once he wrote a girl in reply to a particularly vicious letter that he couldn't pay his bills with anything but money.

He once heard from a man who wrote in one paragraph how great he thought the Bruins were and what a wonderful guy Bobby was, and in the next asked Bobby for five dollars. Orr wrote back that he never sent money to fans. In reply he got a letter reiterating that the Bruins were great but saying that Bobby didn't have any Christmas spirit.

This, of course, was all nothing more than the price of fame. Far more important was the effect Bobby's salary had on his fellow athletes.

Largely because of him, hockey went bigtime overnight, financially as well as in other respects. And that made Bobby Orr a proud and happy young man.

10 The Road Back

Everyone in the Bruins' organization, to say nothing of the thousands of their loyal fans, waited with some apprehension for preseason practice in September of 1968. Not until then would it be known if Bobby's knee were healed.

At first, the worst seemed confirmed. Bobby, obviously favoring his right leg, couldn't skate with the abandon that had made him so great. Not wanting to take any chances, he decided to quit and rest for a week.

During that period he exercised with weights, strengthening the muscles he had not used for months. He came back skating better, though he couldn't skate normally until near the end of training. He didn't play in any exhibition games.

He was the hardest-working man in camp. He did a little more every day until he was in condition and ready for the start of the season. Although still a little apprehensive, he felt sure his troubles were over, at least for the moment.

The real test came on opening night in Boston, when the Bruins faced Detroit at the Garden. Not long after the game started, Gordie Howe came roaring down the ice, deliberately swinging his stick as he passed Orr. Although it hit his left knee squarely, it hardly shook Bobby up.

Making mental note that this was one he wouldn't forget —hockey players always remember an especially hard whack so they can get even when the time comes—Bobby shook it off. The main thing then was that the knee didn't buckle under him.

Later in the game Pete Stemkowski tripped him after an offside whistle. Bobby, relaxed and not expecting the blow, went down in a heap, landing squarely on his left knee.

While fans and Bruins alike held their breath, Orr slowly climbed to his feet, and, as he skated away without limping, the sighs of relief were loud enough to hear.

After the game Coach Harry Sinden of the Bruins raged, "It was a cheap shot by a cheap-shot artist."

But it didn't bother Bobby. He played twenty-five more minutes of the game, taking his regular turn and playing on both the power-play and penalty-killing teams. He then scored the go-ahead goal in a game the Bruins finally won, 4–2.

Although Sinden was upset, Bobby felt no animosity toward Stemkowski or Howe.

"We're all a little sneaky here and there," he remarked. Those guys have a job—to get me. But they're good guys. You really don't find many bad apples in this game."

Orr had a running feud going with Reg Fleming, one of the rougher members of the New York Rangers. It had started in Bobby's rookie year when Fleming speared him in the stomach. Later in the same game Orr dropped him with a stiff body check. From then on, it was war whenever the two met.

In December of 1968, early in a game at New York's Madison Square Garden, Fleming smashed into Orr behind the Bruins' net. Bobby went down, rolled over, then anchored his skates on the ice to get back on his feet.

He put all the weight of his body on his left leg, then strained it further by getting up in a quick movement. There wasn't a hint of pain. Bobby knew then his knee was strong enough for just about anything.

That time Bobby made another mental note—to get Fleming before the night was over. Much later in the game he spotted his quarry at center ice. Orr, holding his stick chest high, skated right at Fleming. When the two collided, it was Fleming who went down; Orr kept his feet.

Instead of being upset, Fleming praised the young Bruins marvel. After the game the Ranger wing said, "He's learned to be mean. He's learned that he has to stand up for his rights in this league. I can't blame him for that."

Bobby *had* to stand up for his rights. There's no tougher team game in the world than big-league hockey. Ability to skate, stick-handle, make plays, score, and try to keep opponents from scoring are only the essentials.

Just as important is the ability to take a beating and to dish one out. Nobody in the NHL was a more natural target than Bobby Orr. The first job the members of any team opposing the Bruins had was to "get" him.

With Orr out of action the Bruins were a different team. The only ways to get him out were either to bait him into an illegal maneuver that would put him into the penalty box or to knock him physically out of the game.

Not long after the 1968–69 season had started, Orr had two fights with Gary Dornhoefer of Philadelphia, who had once played for the Bruins. Dornhoefer deliberately went after him, repeatedly spearing him until Bobby blew his stack.

The first fight landed him in the penalty box for ten minutes. When he returned to the ice and Dornhoefer speared him a few more times, Orr went after him again.

That cost him another major penalty and finished him for the night.

The Flyers went on to win a 4–2 victory over the Orr-less Bruins. There wasn't a doubt in anyone's mind that Dornhoefer's only purpose in heckling Bobby was to get him out of there. His success was an example of how an expansion team can beat a strong contender by getting the right man off the ice.

The pressure on Bobby continued. He was a constant target not only for rival players but sometimes his own fans, too. He never had to worry about the wolves in the stands when he did well at home, but if he messed up a play, the insults came thick and fast.

A crew-cut youngster when he broke into the league, Bobby had begun letting his hair grow. (It later, in accordance with modern fashions, came down over his ears.) Long hair on men annoyed some people, and there were times when those at the Garden let Bobby know it.

The cry "Get a haircut!" became familiar. But it came only when he made a mistake. The rest of the time fans didn't seem to care how long his hair was.

He played when painful, if not serious, injuries might have kept another man on the bench. One night he needed five stitches to sew up a cut on his eye when the puck hit him after he blocked a shot by Jacques Lemaire of Montreal.

By the end of the game, a scoreless tie, the eye was tightly closed and it wasn't much better the following morning. But the Bruins had another game with the Canadiens that night, and since league-leading Montreal was only a point ahead of the Bruins, Orr was badly needed.

Dan Canney, the Bruins' trainer, spent hours applying hot packs to the wound. Some who saw it that afternoon, including even a player or two, thought Orr should go home and rest.

Bobby himself was doubtful, although, as usual, eager to play.

"I don't feel very good," he said. "I wish we didn't have to play. But it's funny. Sometimes you play your best game when you're feeling like this."

While Orr lay on one of the rubbing tables, Turk Sanderson, looking pale and peaked, walked in.

"What's wrong, Turk?" Bobby asked.

"Upset stomach," Sanderson said. "All I've been doing is throwing up."

"You'll score tonight," said Bobby, looking at the sensational young center with his good eye.

"So will you," Sanderson said, and he rushed for the nearest sink.

The two had to be on the ice ahead of time to receive their previous year's awards from Clarence Campbell, the league president. He had come to Boston to present Orr with the Norris Trophy for being the league's outstanding defenseman the previous year and Sanderson with the Calder Trophy for being the outstanding rookie.

Orr could still see out of only one eye when he received his trophy and Sanderson was still sick when he received his. Yet a few minutes later, when the game began, both played as if they were in perfect shape.

The Canadiens were hot at the start and led, 4–1, early in the second period, but the Bruins refused to give up. Once Orr sent Jean Beliveau sprawling, shoving his elbow into Beliveau's face as he went down. Another time he stopped a Lemaire shot with his body.

The Bruins had closed the gap to 4–3 by the end of the second period. Then, early in the third, Sanderson evened the score with the goal Orr had predicted for him. With seven minutes left in the game the score was still 4–4.

93

Suddenly Pie McKenzie passed to Orr on Bruin ice and Bobby flashed past two of the fastest skaters in the league, Henri Richard and Bobby Rousseau, as though they were standing still. He sped across center ice and into Montreal territory, where a Canadiens defenseman, Ted Harris, waited for him.

Harris hit him hard, but Orr was moving so fast the Montreal man couldn't get a square shot at him. Bobby, in fact, was moving too fast. He overskated the slot and, still in possession of the puck, was carried by his own momentum behind the net.

Tony Esposito, then a rookie, who later won fame after being traded in Chicago, was in the Canadiens' goal. He watched closely as Bobby skated first to the right, then to the left, where he could see what he was doing, since his right eye was still closed.

As he swooped around the side of the net, Orr was at such a bad angle that Esposito looked for a pass to center. Instead Bobby saw a small opening between the goalie and the post. He shoveled the puck in backhanded, and the Bruins led, 5–4.

"The guy isn't human," someone murmured on the Canadiens bench.

The Bruins finally won, 7–5, for the game broke wide open after Orr's impossible goal. The victory put them on top of the East division standings.

Later, in the locker room, Orr yelled to Sanderson, "I told you you'd score."

And Sanderson, who had scored twice, retorted, "Seems to me I told you the same thing about yourself."

As he sat in front of his own locker, Sanderson said, "The only thing good about sitting on the bench is that you can watch him all the time. He's the greatest."

On December 16 Bobby collected his first hat trick—

three goals in one game. It was against the Black Hawks at home in the Boston Garden.

The first goal came early in the game, with the Hawks already leading, 1–0. When Pat Stapleton of Chicago went to the penalty box, Coach Harry Sinden of the Bruins inserted his power-play team.

On the face-off Sanderson, a marvel at winning the draw, passed the puck to Eddie Westfall, and the two started down the ice together, with Orr trailing them. Westfall left a drop pass for him as Bobby crossed the Hawks' blue line.

Brushing aside two Chicago penalty killers, Bobby sped into their zone, then smashed the puck so hard from thirty-five feet out that Dave Dryden, the Hawks' goalie, didn't even have time to try to stop the shot with his hand.

It took only five minutes for Bobby to get his second goal of the game. That time he started deep in Bruins territory to make a rush reminiscent of Eddie Shore. As he blew past one Hawks defender after another, featuring the puck in front of him, it was obvious that this would be a one-to-one battle between Orr and Dryden.

After Orr circled the last man in his way, Dryden moved out of his net a few feet and got set for the bullet shot he was sure would come. Instead, with a neat flick of his wrist, Bobby almost casually pushed the puck past the outwitted goalie.

Up in the stands Milt Schmidt, who knew a great play when he saw one, remarked, "You watch him every game and you say you've just seen the best play he ever made. Then you look again and he's doing something better."

Halfway through the second period, Bobby protected a 5–4 Boston lead when Don Awrey was penalized. This time as a penalty killer Bobby filled the role to perfection. He darted all over the ice to keep the Stan Mikita line from scoring for the Hawks.

When that siege ended, Phil Esposito said, "He ought to get the Vezina trophy. He blocks more shots than the goalies."

Esposito sounded like Eddie Johnston, who once said, "I suppose I should give Bobby part of my salary. He does my job better than I do."

The moment Awrey left the penalty box in the Chicago game Orr, still on the ice, took the puck and headed straight for the Hawks' net. After crossing the blue line, he raised his stick and let go with a sizzling slap shot. The harassed Dryden never saw it, and was still wondering how it got into the goal as he fished it out with his big stick.

After a stunned silence of a full second, the 14,653 wildly enthusiastic Boston fans roared one of the warmest receptions the Garden had ever seen. In accordance with custom when someone does a hat trick, hats and caps came flying out of the stands until nearly a hundred were on the ice.

In late December, with the Bruins still challenging the Canadiens for first place, Bobby helped them stay in the fight by doing his part in two victories and a tie out of 3 closely bunched games.

First he set up two key goals to beat St. Louis, 6–2. Then, when the Bruins were trailing Detroit, 3–0, he was in the midst of the action when they scored three times to save the deadlock.

And finally, in New York, he scored the go-ahead goal even though he had spent most of the day in bed nursing a bad cold. Later he prevented a sure goal by Brad Park when he slid on his stomach, reached out with his stick, and deflected a shot that seemed certain to land in the Bruins net. They won that one, 4–2.

The Bruins, reinforced by more new and effective youngsters brought up from farm teams when men were injured, rushed on. Don Marcotte, Wayne Cashman, Rick Smith, and Jim Harrison, tough, hard-driving, and fearless, seemed to fit right into the Bruins picture.

Cashman and Rick Smith were up to stay. Marcotte went back to the minors for more seasoning, but returned to stick the following year. Harrison eventually went to Toronto in a trade for Wayne Carleton.

The Bruins by now had a reputation for toughness unrivaled anywhere in the league. Everyone on the team was so reckless on the ice that *Sports Illustrated* magazine headlined a story called "It's Bobby Orr & The Animals." Bobby's picture was on the cover.

With Teddy Green and Ken Hodge leading the so-called policemen (the toughest men, who protect players belted unfairly or otherwise), the Bruins were known as a club not to be trifled with. For the first time they were the object of a hate campaign, the greatest compliment a pro hockey team can earn.

There never was a great NHL club that everyone else didn't hate. The Bruins of 1968–69 were that type of team, as, indeed, they remained. In hockey, grudging admiration goes hand-in-hand with hatred. The Bruins were, for the first time in years, admired, feared—and hated.

"When they drop the puck to start the game," said Bud Poile, general manager of the Philadelphia Flyers, "the Bruins think it's a piece of raw meat. Do they go after it! I'm afraid my guys will desert the place some night."

One night after the Bruins murdered the Rangers at Madison Square Garden, Coach Boom Boom Geoffrion of the Rangers said, "Never before have I seen a team do what the Bruins did to us tonight."

Coach Punch Imlach of the Maple Leafs, in a desperate attempt to keep the Bruins from getting a fast lead in a game in Boston, started five defensemen against them. Within a couple of minutes there had been eight individual fights and both Teddy Green of the Bruins and Mike Pelyk of the Leafs were in the penalty box.

Imlach's strategy worked, but only for a while. The Leafs scored the first goal of the game, then the Bruins ganged up and won a 5–3 victory.

Bobby Orr was in the middle of all these battles. The young superstar's reputation for toughness had long since been established, and he got into as many fights as his teammates. He had become the symbol of the new Bruins, the anchorman.

With Orr in action the Bruins could do it all. He lent inspiration even while on the bench. Only when he was hurt and completely out of action did they show signs of sagging.

At one time they pulled away from the Canadiens so fast it appeared they would win the Prince of Wales Trophy easily. During that stretch they extended their lead over Montreal to 7 points, but they couldn't hold it. The Canadiens eventually caught and passed them.

But even when the Bruins lost, Orr looked good most of the time. He had his bad nights, but not many. Occasionally his knee swelled up, but rarely to a point where he had to sit out a game.

Everyone marveled at his speed.

"When he goes by my bench," said Imlach, "I turn away so I don't have to watch."

One of Orr's most remarkable attributes was his uncanny ability to do the right thing when he had more than one choice. In enemy territory he usually had two—either to pass the puck or try to score himself.

Invariably he made the proper decision. Even when it failed to work, it was right—obviously *everything* couldn't work. But considering the speed of the action and the tiny flash of time he had to make these decisions, they were amazingly accurate.

Older hockey strategists marveled at his hockey mind.

"The idea is to score goals," one remarked after watching Orr play a great game. "And Bobby knows more about how it should be done than anyone in the game. He seems to act instinctively, almost without thinking. He's like Willie Mays in baseball. You don't have to ask him *why* he does something. He just *knows.*"

The Bruins lost the Eastern division title to Montreal by 3 points, then lost to the Canadiens in the semifinals of Stanley Cup play. From there Montreal went on to an easy cup title, since the expansion St. Louis Blues were their opponents in the finals.

Orr had a great year, breaking a twenty-four-year-old record for defensemen by scoring 21 goals which, with 43 assists, gave him 64 points. The former record of 20 had been set by Flash Hollett of Detroit.

Bobby slumped a bit in the play-offs, scoring 1 goal and 7 assists in 10 games. Nothing to be ashamed of, but it was not up to his usual standard.

But he won the Norris Trophy for the second straight year, and his knee stood up throughout the season. With three fine seasons behind him, the best years of his life were just ahead.

11 A Closely Knit Team

The 1969–70 hockey season began on a sad note for the Bruins. Shortly after the opening of preseason training Teddy Green suffered the depressed skull fracture that knocked him out of action for the year and nearly cost him his life.

No one on the team was more deeply affected by the mishap than Bobby Orr.

As soon as Green was hit, Bobby led the way off the bench in the rush for Wayne Maki, then of the Blues, who had hit Green over the head with his stick. Bobby was completely unnerved by seeing Green rushed away to the hospital. Upon learning of the severity of his friend's injuries, Bobby broke down and cried. Orr was also one of the first Bruins players at the Ottawa Hospital, where the great defenseman hovered between life and death.

He was the first to call Teddy after Green could talk on the telephone. Bobby kept in direct touch with Green by phone once or twice a week all through the season.

As one of the players who suggested that Green be invited to Boston for the Stanley Cup play-off finals, Bobby was in the Bruins group that took Teddy to dinner his first night there since his injury. No wonder that, as with so many other Bruins players, Green considered Orr among his closest friends.

This was part of Orr's particular charisma. He had a genuine interest in the welfare of his teammates, not simply because they were teammates but because they were human beings. They, in turn, felt the same interest in and affection for him.

Another quality of Orr's was his utter lack of personal conceit. His modesty was not a pose, but as real as his sympathy for his fellow man especially others on his own team. He never could understand completely why he got so much credit for the rise of the Bruins from the bottom to the top of the hockey world.

"There are plenty of hockey players as good as I am," he insisted. "And every man on this team has had a hand in our success. I did no more than anyone else."

Orr was neither selfish nor jealous. To Orr no one man deserved to be singled out as being responsible for the Bruins' fine showing as the 1960's ended and the 1970's began.

There might have been friction and jealousy between Orr and Esposito. Because the big center was a master at scoring, he was universally recognized as a superstar very soon after he joined the Bruins. Except for the 1969–70 season Esposito always outscored Orr, which was natural, since no defenseman had ever outscored a center before Bobby. The fact that Orr did it once might have angered Esposito. But there was nothing but warmth and mutual admiration between the two men. The fact that Esposito became the most prolific scorer in the history of the NHL yet did not approach Orr's salary never came between them.

Esposito and Orr were extremely close. Most teams don't

have room for more than one superstar. In the history of sports there have been many examples of two stars on the same team hardly speaking to each other.

Yet not once in the years they were together did a cross or unfriendly word pass between the Bruins' two greatest players. On the contrary, one of the most pleasant pastimes of each was to rib the other. The constant kidding exchange between them livened up locker rooms, airplanes, buses, hotel rooms, and rinks.

Each had tremendous respect for the other and often expressed it. The huge, swarthy, good-natured Esposito and the thinner, shorter, handsome blond never went short of quips and friendly insults when they were together.

Once, after Orr moved to the plush Prudential Center in Boston and invited the Espositos there, Phil said, "It's about time. I was beginning to think you were ashamed of us."

"I'm only ashamed of you," Bobby retorted. "The rest of your family is always welcome here."

They even joked about the discrepancies in their salaries. Eventually Esposito, too, reached the $100,000 level, but at one point after Orr signed his second Bruins contract, the difference between their incomes was just about that much.

Instead of grousing and groaning, Esposito accepted the situation with calm and good grace.

"Bobby deserves every cent he makes," he told others.

But when with Bobby, he rode the youth about his huge salary as hard as everyone else on the team did. And Orr took it all with grins and retorts, never losing his cool or getting upset.

Except for the pall of gloom after Teddy Green's accident —when for a long time it appeared he might be left partially paralyzed—most of what followed in the 1969–70 season was good.

The Bruins were weakend by injuries in the early stages of the season. Green's loss was a heavy blow, for the fiery veteran was an All-Star defenseman and one of the most feared players in the league. And not long after the season began, Turk Sanderson was lost for more than a month. The colorful mod center, a star in his own right, was the best penalty killer and face-off man in the league.

To fill these gaps the Bruins needed help wherever they could get it. The man who gave them more than anyone else was Orr. As great as ever on defense, he went wild on offense, too, piling up goals and assists like mad.

As a result, even without Green, and with Sanderson on the shelf for weeks, the Bruins remained in contention for the East division title. By the first of the year they were only 4 points behind the league-leading Rangers.

"Considering everything that has happened to us so far," said Coach Harry Sinden, "I really couldn't be any happier. Second place looks pretty good right now."

The Bruins certainly didn't owe it *all* to Orr, but it was hard to imagine what would have happened to them if he, too, had been sidelined. He was in his fourth NHL season, and it promised to be his best.

Gerry Cheevers, one of the two regular goalies, expressed what everyone on the club thought when he said, "Here's a kid who's only twenty-one years old and he's keeping us all alive and well. He's got to win the Hart Trophy as the most valuable player, the Norris Trophy as the best defenseman, and the Vezina Trophy as the best goaltender."

"Best goaltender?" an observer asked.

"That's right," Cheevers said. "Bobby has stopped more shots this year than any goalie in the league."

As usual, the praise that was heaped on Bobby's head did not serve to make him conceited, despite his tender years, for he viewed his spectacular actions as just part of his job.

"After four years in the league it's only natural that I've learned some things about people," he said. "I'm wiser now. I handle situations better than I did last year or the year before that. And don't forget, I'm very lucky."

Perhaps he was thinking about Green, and perhaps about himself. He knew Green was at home in Winnipeg, fighting his way back to health. And he could remember all too well the injuries he himself had been fighting during his years in hockey.

The 1969–70 season had truly been free of injuries for Bobby. Except for the normal cuts and bruises that always come in hockey, he had been able to avoid the problems of previous years. His knees were strong and his ability to to avoid serious physical problems contributed to his success.

He maintained his amazing early pace throughout the season. At the midway point his statistics were unbelievable. Of the 103 goals scored against the Bruins by January, Orr had been on the ice for only 42 of them. And of the 131 goals the Bruins had scored by then, Bobby had been on the ice for 88.

He had scored 11 goals and assisted in 45 more for a league-leading total of 56 points, 7 more than Phil Goyette of the Blues, who was then second.

Bobby's points-per-game average halfway through the season was 1.5. If he maintained his pace, his projected total at the end of the season would be 115 points. He actually bettered that mark, with 120. In the fifty-two-year history of the NHL the only other 100-point player was Esposito, who had set his league record of 126 the previous year.

With his knees in good shape Orr could cut and shift and fake even better than ever. He no longer worried about quick changes of pace or direction, with the result that it was impossible for an opponent to anticipate his moves.

"He's like O. J. Simpson on skates," remarked Gary Bergman of the Red Wings.

"He is the fastest and strongest skater the National Hockey League has ever seen," said Jacques Plante of St. Louis, who had been tending goal in it for nearly twenty years.

Phil Esposito, a strong but awkward skater, said of Bobby, "If I could skate like him I'd be All-Week every week of the year."

Sinden thought Orr's newfound scoring touch was the result of his own decision to shoot more and pass less.

"He has a marvelous shot," the Bruins coach said. "It's as fast as anyone's, with the possible exception of Bobby Hull. I've been after him right along to use it, but instead he often gave the puck to someone else when he was deep in the offensive zone. He got a lot of goals but he could have scored many more in the past."

During the season Orr took more shots at the goal than anyone on the team except Esposito, whose job it was to stay near the opposing net for as many shots as he could get. In the first half of that season Bobby took 11 shots in 2 diferent games. This was a high total for anyone, let alone a defenseman.

He was just as prolific at setting up goals. In one game he had 4 assists while taking only 1 shot at the rival nets.

He drove opposing coaches crazy trying to set up defenses against him. They never found one that worked except on the few occasions Bobby had off nights.

"You can't double-team him," said Coach Sid Abel of the Red Wings. "The minute you do, he sees the teammate you left uncovered and hits him with a pass."

Most teams simply put a good forechecker on him and hope for the best. Especially persistent men like Dave Keon of the Leafs, Ralph Backstrom of the Canadiens, or Michel

Briere of the Penguins were assigned to him, but it didn't help much. No matter how good they were at forechecking, they couldn't outskate Bobby.

"He's always isolated when he skates out of our zone," said teammate Don Awrey, who became Orr's defense partner after Green was hurt. "There's never a Bruin near him. He likes plenty of room. This is the first year I worked with him, and it took me a while to keep away from him. Teddy Green and I always used to back each other up, but if you try to do that with Bobby he's gone before you can get started."

Sometimes, especially in Montreal, there were occasional stories trying to prove that Orr's weakness was his heavy concentration on offense, but the hockey players, including the Canadiens themselves, disagreed.

"Sure, he leads the rush," said Gordie Howe of the Wings. "But he's so quick he's the first one back on defense. He does both jobs better than anyone."

Stan Mikita of the Hawks felt the same way: "Bobby thinks defense as long as he's in his own zone and the other team has the puck. But once across his own blue line in possession of the puck, he thinks offense."

Eddie Johnston—who shared the goaltending duties with Gerry Cheevers for the Bruins and, thus, with Cheevers, was in the best position of all to judge Orr's defensive abilities—thought criticism of Bobby in that respect was nonsense.

"He makes hockey a forty-minute game for us," Johnston said. "The other twenty minutes he's got the puck himself, and there isn't any better defense than that."

Bobby Orr shrugged off the whole argument.

"I hear it and read it once in a while," he said, "but it doesn't bother me. Everybody has his own style. Mine's offense."

His rushes from one end of the ice to the other were the most electrifying in hockey. Fans everywhere were on their feet whenever he was off on one.

"Bobby's dynamic," Esposito said. "The fans don't care when I carry the puck or when Jean Beliveau or Stan Mikita or Rod Gilbert have it. But they go crazy when Bobby carries it."

Wherever the Bruins went, fans poured out to see Orr. Like Bobby Hull at the top of his game, he was one man who could fill any arena. Even in Los Angeles, where the expansion Kings had their troubles getting off the ground artistically and financially, Orr packed them in.

One night more than 14,000 went to the Los Angeles Forum to see a game between the Bruins, the best team in the league, and the Kings, the worst. Bobby scored the first and last goals in a 6–2 Bruins victory that night.

Hal Laycoe, later fired as the Kings' coach, said after the game, "These people came to see Orr."

Although the Bruins had four assistant captains (Bucyk, Westfall, Green, and Esposito), the team's acknowledged leader was Orr.

"Bobby never had to say anything to make his leadership felt," said Turk Sanderson. "He has an innate quality that doesn't require words."

Great as he had been in his first three years, Orr reached his peak in the 1969–70 season. Not only his own teammates, but every player in the league marveled at him.

When Gordie Howe was asked what he thought Orr's best move was, the Detroit veteran replied, "Putting on his skates."

Ted Irvine, traded that year in midseason by the Kings to the Rangers, was supposed to be one of the fastest skaters in hockey. But every time he faced Orr, Bobby outskated him.

"He makes you feel as if you're wearing snowshoes," Irvine said.

"He doesn't beat you because he's Bobby Orr" said Glen Sather of the Rangers. "He beats you because he's the best. If he came out in disguise with a wig on his head and different numbers on his back, he'd still beat you."

The Bruins did not win the Prince of Wales Cup, emblematic of the East division NHL championship, but they were second to the Chicago Black Hawks. They then went on to win the Stanley Cup in a virtual sweep, losing only 2 of their 14 play-off games.

In beating the Hawks four straight in the semifinals, the Bruins virtually clinched the title. Throughout the play-offs with the Hawks, Bobby Orr was shadowed by several Chicago players. Orr won the battle so easily that before the semifinals ended the Hawks changed their strategy, but it didn't help them. Orr always found ways to beat them.

Only Phil Esposito outscored Bobby in the play-offs. Orr had 9 goals and 11 assists for 20 points; Esposito had 13 goals and 14 assists for 27. Yet Bobby easily won the Conn Smythe Trophy for being the most valuable man in the play-offs.

It was characteristic of Esposito that he was the first to agree Orr deserved the prize.

"All I do most of the time is stand in front of the other guys' goal waiting for the puck," Esposito said. "But Bobby stops the other team from scoring, *then* comes down the ice to help on offense."

Orr, on the other hand, pointed to Esposito's two play-off years with the Bruins up to that time to show that the big center had taken a bad rap when the Hawks declared he couldn't score in play-offs.

"Who's done any better?" Bobby demanded.

It was a good question. In the 1968–69 play-offs, Esposito had 8 goals and 10 assists for 18 points in the 10 games the Bruins played before they were eliminated. That gave him 21 goals and 24 assists for 45 points in the 24 games in which he took part in two play-off series for the Bruins.

Yet Bobby *was* the Bruins' most valuable player in the 1969–70 Stanley Cup play-offs. They won the cup for the first time since 1941, when a Bruins team anchored by Milt Schmidt had led them to glory.

Two major American sports publications honored Bobby, not only for his Stanley Cup play, but for his work throughout the 1969–70 season.

In naming him "Man of the Year," *Sport* magazine noted: "There have been good seasons, there have been great seasons, and there is the season 21-year-old defenseman Bobby Orr had with the Boston Bruins . . . . It was simply unprecedented. Bobby Orr did things no hockey player ever did before. For his amazing performance, Orr is *Sport*'s Man of the Year."

Sports Illustrated, which had already used Bobby as its cover subject once, did it again when naming him as its Sportsman of the Year. In a headline that amounted to a citation, the magazine noted: "Only 22, he set entire new standards of hockey excellence. While leading his team to a championship and emerging as an all-time star, he ushered a growing sport into the '70's with a flash of flying ice."

It was significant that this was the first time both *Sport* and *Sports Illustrated* had given its highest annual award to a hockey player. It was recognition not only for Orr, but for a professional sport that until he came on the scene had been largely ignored in the United States.

That might have been Orr's greatest contribution to the game he loved.

12 Orr the Man

It is impossible to be a superstar on the American sports scene without undergoing some personality change. Sometimes the change is very evident, sometimes subtle, but it always occurs. Fame alone is often the spur that makes this sort of transformation immediately evident, and what fame doesn't do, money usually does. Bobby was no exception—he changed, for time alone would have changed him. With Bobby the changes of maturity were subtle, as they always are. But the changes resulting from his fame and fortune were perhaps even more subtle.

And this, perhaps, was the most unusual facet of his character. A stranger walking into the Bruins' locker room without knowing what Orr looked like or that he wore number 4 would not have been able to recognize him. Unlike superstars in most sports, he didn't have any more locker space than anyone else. He had no special corner, no room to hide, no armor other than his own ingenuity with which to ward off unwanted visitors.

A professional sports locker room is not a public place. Aside from authorized members of the media, club personnel, or personal friends of the athletes, it is off limits to the general public.

Therefore, athletes can take it for granted that a stranger in the locker room has a good reason for being there. Some enjoy talking to outsiders. Superstars usually are not so quick to welcome them.

The reason is that locker-room visitors are there to ask for something—not money or anything material, but time. The pressure on superstars in this respect is terrific. Every day someone wants a superstar to do something—speak at a banquet, visit a school or a hospital, lend his name to a cause he's never heard of, ask him to write someone, give an autograph, even lend or simply hand out money.

Autographs are easy, and most athletes, superstars or not, comply. But some get uptight even about that. The older and richer and more famous they become, the more unapproachable they are inclined to make themselves.

In some respects Orr became little different from other superstars. He is not so quick to talk to strangers now as he was when he first joined the Bruins. Unless a friend makes the introductions, he is uncommunicative to those he has never met.

He never really got over his fundamental shyness. Although he liked people, he found it hard to make new friends. His relations with the press were generally good, but athletes and writers are natural enemies, as are entertainers and critics.

No writer can cover a major sport honestly without pointing out errors on the field. No athlete, no matter how thick-skinned, likes to have his shortcomings made public. Thus, an honest writer makes a potential enemy every time he criticizes an athlete.

Orr took criticism better than most, but there were writers Orr didn't like. He rarely showed his dislike by arguing or even trying to reason. His method was simply to clam up. The best he would do was answer yes or no to every question or, if he didn't want to say anything, "No comment."

His shyness kept him from saying much at the start of his professional career, and his distrust had the same effect once he was established. In this, he was no different from any other athlete. But in several ways he was different from other superstars.

He could be what the press calls a "good interview" if the questions were straightforward and the writers weren't looking for a story that might hurt someone.

Throughout his career Bobby Orr has never been known to criticize the ability of another athlete. He might criticize a rival for taking a cheap shot at him, but only in the heat of the moment. He learned eventually to say something like, "Don't print this but—"

Even then, he had to know the interviewer. If he didn't, he said nothing.

He learned his obligation to fans long before most superstars do. He realized he was—to hockey fans at least—a public figure. He would like to preserve his private life, but that isn't always possible.

Certain subjects—such as his income, his family, his private life, his business dealings, and his personal habits— he never discusses. Nor does he go into such matters as his dress, his hair, his friends, or anything else he feels is nobody's business but his.

Therefore, if any member of the media tries to pry information from him on these subjects, he quickly excuses himself and turns the other way. An ordinary athlete would not have been blamed for taking this attitude.

But a superstar is always under the spotlight. Anything anyone can find out about him is presumed by some as public property. Orr understandably didn't agree.

It took years, but eventually he had a reputation for being hard to talk to. In a way it was deserved, but not for the reason most potential interviewers thought.

He was just a quiet guy. He was quiet when he first joined the Bruins and he continued to be quiet throughout his career. Only with family and close friends did he open up to a point where he would initiate a discussion. With others he had to be asked.

He liked the same things other young men liked—girls, fun, good food, and beer. He minded his own business and hoped others would mind theirs. He was courteous, good-hearted, and willing to help less fortunate people. He made many more friends than enemies. He was not a clown, a character, or a colorful personality. In general he let his actions on the ice do the talking for him.

He followed the crowd in his appearance. The brush cut at eighteen became the long hair at twenty-three. His clothes were the clothes of his fellows—not extremely mod but not old-fashioned either.

In appearance he never completely lost the little-boy look he had brought with him from Parry Sound to Boston. As the years passed, his profession began showing on his still-pleasant face—thick tissues over the eyes, facial scars from flying pucks and swinging sticks, an irregular nose, lips thickened by frequent stitches.

Injuries are routine in hockey, brutality a way of life. Orr, in the middle of it for years, was, like his friend Teddy Green, gentle off the ice, tough on it.

He rarely refuses a request involving the sick, the maimed, the mentally retarded. He once let a retarded boy use his gloves in a pickup game at a school for the mentally defective. When the game ended, the boy threw the gloves into Bobby's face and said, "I don't like you."

As he walked away, Bobby looked at him and shook his head.

"Poor kid," he murmured. "He doesn't know what he's doing."

His lawyer and close friend, Alan Eagleson, often calls him a bleeding heart. Eagleson once told Jack Olsen of *Sports Illustrated* that he gives so much away, endorses so many bonuses and checks for appearances and the use of his name over to the clergy for the poor and the orphaned that neither Bobby nor his attorney can keep track of them. Although not a Catholic, he gave thousands to priests working with the underprivileged.

He served as chairman of all sorts of charitable drives, both in the United States and Canada. His interest always went beyond the use of his name. He visited the afflicted to see for himself what they had to go though—and to cheer them up.

Only Ted Williams, another Boston athlete, was less inclined to disclose the charitable nature of his outside activities. The onetime Red Sox baseball star reveled in his reputation as a difficult personality, but he was as gentle as a nurse with the sick and as generous as a philanthropist with the poor.

Frosty Foristall, the Bruins assistant trainer, with whom Orr lived in Boston for years before he was married, gave Olsen a typical picture of the human side of Bobby Orr.

"It's reached a point where something's got to give," Foristall said. "It either gotta be his play or his charities. Every time I turn around in the apartment there's five kids from Cerebral Palsy and a photographer, and it's time to go to the game and Bobby's saying, 'No, no, no hurry, this is more important,' and he'll sit there forever with those kids."

No matter how much Orr ever makes, money never

means anything. He spent little on himself, mostly because he did not want to set himself apart from his teammates. He always kept himself financially on the level of the people he was with.

And in this he was considerably different from most superstars. Knowing they are in higher money brackets than their fellows, they often feel an obligation to pick up checks, to spend their social hours with their financial equals.

In some cases this has caused incongruities because a sports superstar is in a younger age bracket than a mature man who has made big money in some other field. The result is the average superstar's best friends are considerably older than he is.

With Orr this is not the case. His friends are mostly other hockey players, especially teammates, or people with whom he grew up in Parry Sound. He did not have unlimited funds as a boy, which may be one reason he never spent unlimited funds when he got into high income brackets.

"He is entirely unmotivated by any personal desire for money," Eagleson told Olsen. "If he doesn't want to do something, he won't do it no matter what the money. I have him on an allowance of about twenty thousand a year, and he kicks back maybe half of it unused. He makes a quarter of a million a year *off* the ice—endorsements and private deals and things—and I'm not saying how much on the ice. He'll be a millionaire in a few years, and he couldn't care less."

Orr told Olsen about Deanna Deleidi, a steady Bruins fan who rarely misses a game at the Boston Garden.

"She goes home to an iron lung every night," Bobby said, "and still gives me a kiss and a hug after every hockey game. All I have to do is see someone like that and then I don't think I'm such a big hero anymore."

116

One of Bobby's teammates describes his charitable activities almost as though they were an affliction.

"He's been too good, and he better cut it out," the player said. "He's even given money to some hockey players. He thinks it's a loan, but it's a gift. He'll never see it again. All this running around to mental hospitals and VA hospitals and poor people's parishes—it's gonna start showing up in the ice, in his play. This is his big problem, the way other people have problems with liquor or dope or women."

After practice and sometimes after games Orr went to a bar near the Garden where he and the bartender spent hours figuring ways for Bobby to help others. The bartender, Tommy Maher, always had half a dozen little autographing chores, mostly for children or the sick or the old or the poor. While Maher spelled out names or dictated short notes, Bobby wrote everything down and signed it.

Orr never threw away used equipment, nor did he give it away indiscriminately. Most of it went to Maher, who auctioned it off. Once the bartender sold a pair of Bobby's skates for thousand dollars for a youth center in an underprivileged area.

Bobby uses luxury cars literally forced on him by local automobile dealers. Ordinarily he accepted only three— one for himself, one for friends, and one for his father in Parry Sound. He takes these only because the donors insisted.

Snowmobile dealers even gave the Orr family enough vehicles to take care of all who wanted them during the heavy Parry Sound winters. A Boston furrier once tried to get Bobby to accept a full-length mink coat, but he refused. He just couldn't see himself going around in a mink coat.

His carelessness about money sometimes drives Eagleson up the wall. Bobby doesn't waste money—he just forgets what he has. He once carried a check for $11,000 from January to June before giving it to Eagleson, who handles all his investments.

Whether or not he accepted a request for an appearance never had any relation to what he might be paid. One night he might go somewhere for nothing and the next turn down an offer of five thousand dollars. Even when he accepts money, he often gives it away, sometimes to his philanthropic bartender friend, sometimes to a welfare worker or a member of the clergy.

He gave more to the Catholic clergy in Boston because more Catholics were there and more priests and nuns were working with the poor. Often the work is ecumenical, which Bobby knew and appreciated.

Not only is Orr a remarkable hockey player, but a remarkable humanitarian. No one was ever more thankful for God-given talents and few ever did more to express their thanks.

Yet he never asked for credit, nor even talked about the things he did for others. If he had his way, it would all remain a secret between him and the recipient.

In that way he is much like Ted Williams, but there the resemblance stops. Williams was difficult and unpredictable, a man who could strike fear and awe into the hearts of even his own teammates. Orr never wanted anyone to hold him in fear or awe. All he wanted was the respect and friendship of those with whom he had contact.

He got both.

13   Collapse of Giants

In many ways the 1970–71 Bruins season was the most astounding in the entire history of professional hockey. It began with a curious twist and ended in complete frustration, yet during the season itself the Bruins set more team and individual records than the pro game has ever seen.

The curious twist approached the bizarre in nature when Harry Sinden resigned as coach the day after the club won the Stanley Cup to climax the 1969–70 season. The only sports incident that compared with it was Manager Johnny Keane's resignation from the St. Louis Cardinals right after they won the 1964 World Series.

But there was one big difference. Keane remained in baseball, succeeding Yogi Berra as the New York Yankees manager. Sinden got out of hockey altogether.

From later disclosures it became apparent that Sinden had decided long before the season ended to resign, and that a salary hassle with the club was his principal motivation. Whether or not this was true, there were no hard feelings,

119

for two years later the young coach returned as the Bruins general manager.

His resignation as coach in 1970 came as a shock to everyone, especially the players, with whom Sinden was very popular. All, including Bobby Orr, considered him a combination of friend, personal adviser, and team strategist.

Because of his own youth, he could identify with the young, effervescent man who had brought the Stanley Cup to Boston under his direction. The harmony between players and coach had been an important factor in this victory.

On the other hand, the talent was so rich that many, players included, once they got over the shock of Sinden's departure, felt that the team could win with almost any coach of reasonable competence. The Bruins truly looked like the baseball Yankees of old, who made one manager after another look like a genius.

Thus, whoever replaced Sinden was on the spot. It's impossible to improve on a championship record. Sinden's successor could well be as able as Sinden, but if he didn't win the Stanley Cup, he stood the risk of being considered a failure.

The man who moved into this unenviable situation was Tom Johnson. A mild-mannered, forty-two-year-old member of hockey's Hall of Fame with a penchant for wearing bow ties, Johnson had spent fifteen years as an outstanding defenseman in the National Hockey League.

All but the last few of those years were with the Canadiens. Johnson finished his career in Boston, where he was Teddy Green's defense partner until he suffered a severed leg nerve when cut by a rival's skate.

Although that ended his playing career, Johnson stayed in hockey via the Bruins' front office. A personable man with a keen eye for a promising hockey player, he worked himself up to assistant general manager.

It was from that job that he was appointed coach. The move was popular with the players, all of whom knew him well, but Johnson still had to prove himself. He had never coached before.

Orr was one of the hardest-hit when Sinden left, because he and Sinden had started with the club together. Perhaps one reason Johnson was named Sinden's successor was that Bobby knew and liked him.

There was no question that Orr would have been great under anybody. But the fact that his new coach was not a stranger to him was helpful. Bobby would miss Sinden, but he accepted Johnson with more enthusiasm than he might have accepted a total newcomer to the Bruins' scene.

The most poignant feature of preseason training at London, Ontario, in the early autumn of 1970 was the return of Teddy Green. Having weathered his terrible ordeal and through sheer perseverance and desire worked himself back into shape, Green had won the admiration of players and fans throughout the hockey world.

Although they later had their differences, Johnson handled Green with patience and consideration in the early months of the season. As always, Bobby Orr led the Teddy Green cheering section, which included the rest of the team.

Bobby was one of the first to welcome Green back into the Bruins fold. The day never went by without an encouraging word to Green from the youthful superstar.

With the wisdom of a much older man Orr extended no sympathy—Green didn't want that and Bobby knew it— but showed his respect in the affectionately rough manner of all men who take part in a risky contact sport.

He rode Green, called him crazy names, and along with his teammates exchanged insults with the former All-Star defenseman starting the uphill road back.

It was, in fact, another example of the Orr charisma

and the amazing empathy the twenty-two-year old spiritual leader of the Bruins had for his fellow man. While not letting Green feel sorry for himself, Orr made it immediately apparent to Teddy that he sympathized, yet expected Green to make it back on his own.

This was a quality that made Orr someone very special in the professional sports world. Without being a Nice Nellie or a Pollyanna, Orr exuded warmth and understanding, both of which were tremendously helpful to Green.

The Bruins, highly favored by experts, fans, and even rivals to win everything, ripped through a season of unprecedented successes. With Tom Johnson skillfully guiding them in his quiet way, they were far and away the class of the league, just as everyone had expected.

They made a shambles of the East Division race, not only as a team but as a collection of outstanding hockey players. The figures the Bruins piled up collectively and individually were awesome.

Not even in the great days of the Canadiens, who won more Stanley Cups than any other NHL team, were so many men so overwhelmingly superior to their peers.

Orr and Esposito led the way, of course. Both were at the top of the heap in almost all offensive departments and, as usual, Orr was the best defenseman in the league. The combination of these two superstars seemed to inspire their teammates to greater heights than ever.

Still a rough, tough team that was often criticized for its merciless methods of attack, the Bruins had class, too. Never did a team have so many players so close to the top in so many facets of the game.

Orr had another typically amazing season. For the second year in a row he played in all the Bruins games, which meant he remained free of serious injury. Thanks to his health, he won another imposing collection of awards.

The Norris Trophy for being the outstanding defenseman in the league went to Bobby for the fourth straight year. His 37 goals broke his own league record for defensemen, which had been 33.

He became the first player ever to collect 100 or more assists when he piled up 102. The record he broke—his own, of course—had been 87.

For the second straight season he won the most significant of all NHL awards, the Hart Trophy for being the league's most valuable player.

And a new honor came his way when he was named the winner of the Lou Marsh Trophy for being the outstanding athlete in Canada. This, of course, embraced all sports and gave added luster to his own country's national game.

Everything Orr did contributed to both the team and individual totals, which were the most impressive of all time. The Bruins, in winning the Prince of Wales Cup for the East division title, won a record 57 games and scored a record 121 points, 12 more than the second-place Rangers. The club also scored a record 399 goals.

On February 25, 1971, the Bruins set an unusual record by scoring 3 goals in 20 seconds, the fastest 3 goals in NHL history. It happened in the third period of a game against Vancouver, with Johnny Bucyk, Eddie Westfall, and Teddy Green doing the scoring. The fact that Green was involved was a source of satisfaction to everyone.

The Bruins broke another unusual record when they scored 25 goals while shorthanded. These, of course, were all registered by what was supposed to be the penalty-killing team. The significance of that mark can best be appreciated by the fact that it nearly doubled the old record of 14, held by the Chicago Black Hawks.

Between February 23 and March 20, 1971, the Bruins

123

had the longest winning streak of the year when they took 13 games in a row.

The club feat of breaking the record for total goals also gave it a new record for assists, with 697, and total points, 1,096. No NHL team had ever collected 1,000 scoring points in one season.

The Bruins plastered the whole league in individual scoring honors. The prolific Esposito broke a couple of his own league records with 76 goals and 152 points. He led the way to the most astounding blanketing of the league a single team ever made.

The top 4 men led the league in points—Esposito with 152, Orr with 139, Bucyk with 116, and Hodge with 105. The Bruins also had the seventh man in Wayne Cashman and the eighth in Johnny McKenzie. For good measure Fred Stanfield was tied with 2 others for ninth.

Almost lost in these great figures was the fact that the Bruins became the first team to have 2 men with more than 50 goals; along with Esposito's 76 went Bucyk's 51.

After a dream season like that, the Bruins were top-heavy favorites to defend their Stanley Cup championship successfully. And therein lies the tale of the complete frustration in which they ended the season.

The man who did them in was a tall rookie goalie named Ken Dryden. A law student at McGill, Dryden had spent most of the season with the Montreal Canadiens' top farm club, the Voyageurs, who also played in Montreal. By the time the Stanley Cup play-offs began, Dryden had played in only six National Hockey League games.

Six feet four inches tall, with, apparently, ice water instead of blood running through his veins, Dryden, a Cornell graduate, calmly led the Canadiens all the way to the cup.

His first victims were the Bruins, who didn't get beyond the quarter-finals.

The Bruins, themselves, hardly knew what hit them. Bobby Orr got them off to the right start when he beat Dryden on a wicked shot from the blue line before the first game was four minutes old.

It appeared as if the rest would be easy. The Canadiens had lost 5 of their 5 regular-season games to the Bruins and had been murdered twice in their last week of the season. Bringing Dryden up from the Voyageurs had been a desperation measure. When Orr beat him so quickly for the first score of the game, Dryden's promotion seemed a wasted gesture.

Orr dominated the game. Under his leadership, which included almost a one-man job of penalty killing, the Bruins won a 3–1 victory. Costarring with Bobby was Gerry Cheevers, who played a fantastic game in the nets.

But there was a couple of jarring notes for the Bruins. One was the fact that Dryden made some marvelous stops himself, giving notice that beating him would not be easy.

The other was a sudden display of temper on Bobby's part, which nearly got him thrown out of the play-offs altogether.

When referee John Ashley penalized Bobby for holding Yvan Cournoyer of the Canadiens, Orr blew his stack. As he skated beside Ashley on his way to the penalty box, Bobby yelled, "You miss fourteen penalties and then call a cheap one on me."

He made a few more choice remarks insulting enough for Ashley to tack on a ten-minute misconduct penalty. By then, Bobby had already reached the box. Furious, he jumped out, pushed Ron Ego, a linesman, out of the way, and headed for Ashley.

With Orr so mad he hardly knew what he was doing, everyone in the Boston Garden realized that if he should lay a hand on Ashley, he could be thrown out of the play-offs.

So Garden customers were treated to the unusual sight of six of Bobby's teammates descending on him at once. Rick Smith actually punched him in the chest to get him back to the boards and into the penalty box again.

Later Bobby apologized profusely while Ashley suddenly played dumb. No, he hadn't seen Bobby leave the box. No, he hadn't seen Bobby shove Ego. No, he didn't have any idea that Bobby was on his way toward him.

That was all that saved the Bruins from losing the services of their star for the rest of the series. But the fact that he could become so incensed was disturbing. More than one Bruins fan wondered what effect the incident might have on future Stanley Cup games.

But the next night there seemed nothing to worry about. The Bruins piled up an early 5–1 lead. With Eddie Johnston in their nets, they appeared well on their way to their second straight quarter-final victory.

In the second period Henri Richard stole the puck from Orr and slammed it into the Bruins' net. Johnston didn't have a chance, and the score was 5–2 Bruins. It held up through the rest of the period.

Jean Beliveau, then thirty-nine years old and one of the last vestiges of the great Canadiens teams of the past, scored a power-play goal early in the third period. That made it 5–3. A few minutes later, with both teams back at full strength, Beliveau beat Johnston again, and the Bruins lead was shaved to 5–4.

While the partisan Boston fans watched in horror, Jacques Lemaire suddenly broke through the Bruins' defense and fired in the tying goal. Now the Bruins had blown a 4-goal lead, and the third period wasn't over yet.

With minutes left to play, Beliveau passed a backhander to teammate John Ferguson, who flicked the puck past Orr and Johnston, and the Canadiens moved into a 6–5 lead.

Just before the final buzzer Frank Mahovlich added insult to injury by breaking through and scoring Montreal's seventh goal of the night.

It was probably the worst thirty minutes of Orr's NHL career. Besides letting Richard steal the puck from him in the second period, he had given it up to Ferguson, who passed to Beliveau for the ancient star's second goal of the third session.

Bobby had been on the ice for 6 of the 7 Montreal goals, but he was not alone among the erring Bruins. Johnston, while making some fine stops, hardly covered himself with glory in the nets. Esposito had been held scoreless. And the whole Bruins team, once in the long lead, had obviously let down.

Although the series was tied and the Bruins were far from out of it, that second game was the turning point. The following Saturday, with Dryden looking like a spider as he made miraculous stops with arms and legs as well as body, the Canadiens moved into the lead.

A hat trick by Bobby, the first for a defenseman in forty-four years in Stanley Cup play, gave the Bruins a 5–2 victory in the fourth game and tied the series again, but that was the last great offensive gesture for Boston.

With Dryden performing wondrous, almost unbelievable, feats in the Montreal goal, the Canadiens eliminated the Bruins in one of hockey's greatest upsets. They then went on to win the Stanley Cup, since the other teams they faced could do no more with the remarkable rookie goalie than had the Bruins.

Despite his one bad game, Orr had a good Stanley Cup series. In the 7 games against the Canadiens he had 5 goals and 7 assists for 12 points, outscoring even Esposito, whose 3 goals and 7 assists gave him 10 points.

Of more significance was Bobby's penalty total. In the 7 games he spent 25 minutes in the box, more than a quarter of the time he had spent there during the whole regular season. In that stretch he was penalized only 91 minutes in 78 games, an average of a little over a minute per game.

With the 1971 season over it would normally have been contract time again. That was Bobby's fifth season with the Bruins. His first contract had been for two years, the second for three. Now Alan Eagleson and Charles W. Mulcahy, Jr., representing the club, were ready to sit down and work out a new pact for Eagleson's famous client—as far as the press and public knew.

What nobody except the principals knew was that Orr and the Bruins had already come to terms after lengthy negotiations. On February 14 at the Royal York Hotel in Toronto Bobby signed the richest contract ever given an NHL player.

The terms were not announced until the following September. Then, at a big press conference in Boston, it was disclosed that Bobby had signed a contract for $1,000,000 spread over five years. That was $200,000 a season, not only more than any hockey player had ever received up to that time, but more than any Boston professional athlete had ever commanded.

"I don't think any other individual has helped to hike salaries in his sport the way Bobby has," Eagleson said. "Maybe with the exceptions of Arnold Palmer in golf and Babe Ruth in baseball, nobody has done more to raise pay scales in any sport."

Aside from the actual amount and length of the contract, nothing more was ever announced either by the Bruins or Bobby. However, it was known that the pact included many fringe benefits, including deferred payments for tax purposes.

Later it was disclosed that Eagleson and Mulcahy had begun negotiations about a year before they were completed.

As Eagleson said, "We signed on Valentine's Day, and it was a sweetheart of a contract."

14   Back on the Beam

The world's highest paid hockey player started slowly when the 1971–72 NHL season got under way, and the Boston fans didn't like it. Perhaps he was saving himself for the clutch games that would come later. Or perhaps he didn't want to hog the spotlight or seem to take attention away from his teammates.

Whatever the reason, Orr played defensive hockey in the early stages of the season. He rushed very little, perferring to hang back and be a true defenseman. In that capacity he was, as in so many other capacities, in a class by himself, but that wasn't the Bobby Orr the fans paid their money to see.

He emerged from his defensive shell suddenly, and, once out of it, he stayed out and ripped his way through another sensational season. It was almost as if he were trying to atone for the Bruins' failure to win their second straight Stanley Cup the year before.

The summer following that collapse had been a tough one for all the Bruins. Wherever they went, they were forced to hear the same bewildered question—"What happened?"

Weston Adams, Jr., the club president, heard it. Milt Schmidt, the general manager, heard it. Tom Johnson, the coach, heard it. And of the players, all of whom were plagued by it, no one heard it more often than Bobby Orr.

"Nobody ever asked me how we did during the season," Bobby said. "Only what happened to us in the play-offs."

The only answer any of the Bruins could give was, "Ken Dryden." The tall rookie Canadiens goalie certainly hadn't won the cup all by himself, but he was largely responsible for the Bruins' not winning it.

The fact that they didn't reflected more on Bobby than on any of his teammates. Even Tom Johnson, whose first year as coach had been all but wrecked by the Stanley Cup fiasco, didn't take the verbal beating that Orr did.

Some observers even went so far as to question his ability as a winner.

"Maybe," one wrote in a national publication, "he's like Ted Williams—a winner for himself but not for the team."

That was the unkindest cut of all, for Bobby had already proved he was a team man and a winner for everyone, not just himself. After all, the Bruins *had* won the 1970 Stanley Cup. All that stopped them from repeating was an unusually hot streak by a young goalie.

The repeated embarrassing question, the hints that Bobby was more for himself than the team, the doubts cast on the greatness of the Bruins, the questions raised by the unexpected change of coaches, all had some bearing on the club that reported for preseason training in the early autumn of 1971.

Actually the team was stronger than ever. Ace Bailey, up

132

from Oklahoma City to stay after several previous unsuccessful attempts, was rapidly becoming a polished left wing. Mike Walton, acquired the season before in a trade with Toronto, added class to an already classy collection of centers.

One disappointing feature was Tom Johnson's failure to stick with Teddy Green. Green's amazing comeback of the year before had ended on a sour note when Johnson went cold on him. Now Johnson continued to use Green sparingly. He was the fifth defenseman almost from the start of the season. Orr, Awrey, and Rick and Dallas Smith, were all considered ahead of him.

Green was never again a strong factor in the Bruins' scheme of things. Midway through the 1971–72 season the Bruins sent Rick Smith and two others to California for Carol Vadnais and Don O'Donoghue. Vadnais was an outstanding defenseman. O'Donoghue was a promising young wing whom the Bruins immediately sent to their Boston farm club, the Braves.

Vadnais was the key man. Once he arrived with the Bruins, there was little hope of Green playing much at all. As it turned out, the Bruins didn't protect him in the 1972 player draft. Since he was on the last season of a three-year contract, he signed with the new World Hockey Association's Boston team.

In the meantime Orr had become stronger as the season wore on. By continuing to avoid serious injury almost up to the last minute of the regular season, he added more accomplishments to his amazing career.

He and Phil Esposito gave the East team a 3–2 victory over the West in the twenty-fifth annual NHL All-Star game. It was Bobby's fifth such game and Esposito's fourth, but the first in which Orr had starred. Up to then he hadn't scored a point in All-Star competition.

133

In February, while Bobby was going at his best pace of the year, he took a whack on his left knee from Bobby Clarke of the Philadelphia Flyers. Although it didn't knock him out of action, it bothered him for the rest of the year.

When a hockey player sustains an injury, the only way to learn how serious it might be is to give him a thorough examination. Most players won't admit they're hurt until they can't play at all, and Bobby was no exception.

As a matter of fact, his tolerance of pain and his refusal to quit in the face of it was one of his greatest assets. Everyone accepted it as fact that the knee bothered him only a bit for the remainder of the season.

In view of what happened later, it was probable that he played in intense pain—at times on only one leg—most of the year from the Clarke injury on. Then, in the last week of the season, he aggravated the injury when he was hit by Dan Johnson of Detroit.

After that he made no attempt to hide the pain, but he still refused to quit. Throughout the season the Bruins played 78 games. Bobby missed only 2 of them.

In almost any other sport he would have missed at least a couple of weeks after the first injury, and he surely would have been out for the year after the second.

But the Bruins faced Stanley Cup competition by then, and the last thing Bobby wanted was to miss any of those pressure games. In his view as well as in the view of everyone else connected with the Bruins, it was his and the club's only chance to redeem themselves after the debacle of the play-offs the year before.

It was a minor miracle that Orr got through the regular season at all, and a major one that he took such an active part in the 1972 Stanley Cup play-offs.

His season's records would have been outstanding under

any circumstances. But considering the condition of his knee, they were virtually unbelievable.

The Bruins swept the board, including a Stanley Cup triumph that gave them two in three years. And without Bobby Orr, injured knee and all, they couldn't have done it.

The only reason Orr didn't establish more records was that he had done that the previous year. But in almost every department he came so close it was almost a certainty that with a sound knee he would have exceeded practically all the league marks he had previously set.

He tied his own league record, 37, in goals scored by defensemen. His 80 assists, the third highest total of his career, led the league for the third straight year. His 117 point total was also his third highest. He still remained the only NHL defenseman in history to exceed 100 points.

For the fifth straight year Orr won the Norris Trophy for being the league's outstanding defenseman. This made him only the second player to win the same award five years in a row. His lone predecessor was Jacques Plante, winner of the Vezina Trophy for being the best goalie in the five seasons between 1956 and 1960.

When Bobby won the Hart Trophy for being the league's most valuable player, he became the first to take it three years in succession. And when he captured the Smythe Trophy for being the outstanding man in the Stanley Cup play-offs, he became the first to win that coveted award twice.

To add even more prestige Bobby scored the goal that clinched the Stanley Cup for the second time in three years. In the whole history of Stanley Cup play, which extends well beyond the formation of the NHL, Orr was only the fourth man to score 2 winning Cup goals.

His insistence on going through the grueling Stanley Cup

135

play-offs with a knee that required surgery undoubtedly saved the cup for the Bruins.

Nobody could have stopped Orr from playing, least of all his coach, Tom Johnson.

"All I know," Johnson said, "is that Bobby *says* he's all right. The swelling on his knee has gone down and he says he's never been better. But who knows with that guy? If he says he's ready, who's going to argue with him? Not me."

All through the play-offs Orr needed daily treatment and a pressure pack on his knee. Occasionally he winced in pain, but refused to miss a turn on the ice. He knew he was needed, he wanted to play, and that was that.

And how he played! In the 15 games the Bruins needed to win their second Stanley Cup in three years, he led everyone in assists, with 19, and was tied with Phil Esposito for first place in total points, with 24. And he assisted the great Bruins scorer on almost all of Esposito's 9 goals.

Sport magazine, in presenting Orr with a new Dodge Charger for his role as the most valuable player in the final round of Stanley Cup play, described Bobby's performance against the Rangers:

"[Orr] was at his best when his best was needed. Playing against the Rangers on a damaged knee that would require post-play-off surgery, Bobby scored, fed, checked, killed penalties, started rushes and logged more ice time than anyone.

"In the six games against New York he scored four goals and four assists. He won the important fourth game, on New York ice, almost by himself with a two-goal performance. And in the sixth game, again in New York, it was all Orr.

"Midway in the first period, he took a pass at the point, feinted Bruce MacGregor with a classic pirouette and rifled a 40-footer into the Rangers' net.

136

"In the final period, with the score 1–0 and the outcome still very much in doubt, Orr blasted another shot from the blue line. It struck Wayne Cashman's stick and slithered into the nets."

Since the Bruins won that final game, 3–0, all they needed was Bobby's first goal. That gave them the series and the cup, 4 games to 2.

In reaching the finals the Bruins lost only 1 game in 2 preliminary series. They took 4 out of 5 from Toronto in the quarter-finals, then swept four games from St. Louis in the semifinals.

To say Orr—or even Orr and Esposito—won the cup would be hardly fair to the rest of the Bruins team. Johnny Bucyk, Ken Hodge, and Esposito each scored 9 goals; Bucyk and Hodge were third and fourth behind the two superstars in total points.

John McKenzie and Fred Stanfield were sixth and seventh; Mike Walton and Wayne Cashman were also among the scoring leaders in the series. Altogether the Bruins had more than half of the 15 leaders—8 men.

This was without respect to the remarkable job turned in by their two goalies—Eddie Johnston and Gerry Cheevers. Between them they had 3 shutouts, 2 1-goal games and 6 2-goal games, all of which the Bruins won.

In the final game, with six seconds to play and the Bruins home free with their 3–0 lead, Ken Hodge passed the puck to Orr. It was a typical tribute to a remarkable hockey player.

Hodge, like all his teammates, was well aware how much Bobby meant to the Bruins. By giving Bobby the puck, Hodge was saying in effect, "you should have it when the game ends."

He might have added, "Nobody in the whole series has had it as much."

Bobby grinned as he took the pass. Leisurely he turned in a wide circle as he watched the big clock at the opposite end of the rink tick away the seconds.

Even the Rangers understood the significance of his possession of the little black disc. Three goals behind, with the last seconds slipping away, nobody on the New York club tried to take the puck from Bobby—as if anyone could have. The Rangers, too, felt he should have it when the final buzzer sounded.

Their captain, Vic Hadfield, later expressed the feelings, not only of his own club but of the entire National Hockey League when he said of Orr after the game, "The guy always had the puck. And when he had it, there wasn't a thing we could do about it."

Derek Sanderson, Bobby's flamboyant teammate, added a tribute of his own by saying, "Bobby controlled the puck for forty minutes and was nice enough to let the other thirty-five players in the game use it for the other twenty."

Despite his great season and play-off series Orr and the Bruins were apprehensive about his left knee. There seemed no doubt that surgery was essential, which Bobby himself accepted as inevitable.

In fact, he was more in favor of an operation than others connected with the Bruins. A few of those opposed to surgery pointed to Bobby Hull as a classic example of a superstar with a bad knee who consistently refused surgery yet starred year after year for his team.

Orr, on the other hand, cited his own previous operations as the only answer to his knee problems.

"I don't know anything about Hull's knee condition," he said one day. "All I know is that if I hadn't let doctors open the knee before, I wouldn't be playing now. I played before with unbearable pain, and I had plenty of that this year, especially during the play-offs. Surgery seems to be the only answer for me—my only hope to keep going."

Perhaps it was only hope, perhaps not. After all, Orr was still only twenty-four, an age when many professionals were just breaking into the NHL. Yet by that time he had spread-eagled the whole league for six years.

He still had a long way to go. If Hull's knee condition righted itself, why shouldn't Orr's? Whatever the situation, Bobby was determined to have surgery; he was operated on within a few weeks of the Stanley Cup play-offs.

Despite previous troubles with the knee, it was only the third operation. Both the other two had been in Orr's second NHL season after he had hurt the knee in the Winnipeg charity game that summer.

Dr. Carter Rowe, one of the top orthopedic surgeons in the country, operated on Bobby in early June at Massachusetts General Hospital in Boston. Later Dr. Rowe issued an optimistic statement, in which he said Orr should be "back on skates and ready for training camp in September."

He later added, "This was an overall cleanup operation. I foresee no problems. Several portions of the knee cartilage were removed and spurs also were removed from the inner knee."

Bobby himself was overoptimistic, for he thought he would be ready for the 1972 late-summer series that had been arranged between All-Star teams from Canada and Russia. If he had been, the results of that series might have been different.

Team Canada, made up of NHL stars, expected an easy time in the 8 scheduled games. But with Orr still on the shelf the Canadians had to fight for their lives. Instead of an easy time they came within a game of losing the series.

Only a great performance by Phil Esposito saved the NHL

stars. Orr, only beginning to skate, sat out the whole series (although he went to Russia with the team).

So for the NHL the 1972 season ended on an unhappy note. Instead of proving themselves undeniably the greatest hockey players in the world, their men were barely able to save face.

But for the Boston Bruins in general and Bobby Orr in particular, the season was a resounding success. With 2 Stanley Cup championships in 3 years the team proved its greatness, and Orr proved as great a team player as he was an individual.

15 "Doing More by Doing Less"

The autumn of 1972 was the most frustrating time in Bobby Orr's remarkable NHL career. His knee problems forced him into the uncomfortable role of spectator role of spectator during the Team Canada/Soviet Union National team series and restricted his performance throughout the 1972–73 NHL season.

Badly overweight at 213 pounds, Orr started to skate during Team Canada's training camp in early August. There was considerable speculation that he would be ready to play in the games at Moscow in late September.

"I was really worried about my knees and my future," Orr said. "Hockey is my life, and you can't survive for very long with a poor knee. Boy, did I want to play against those Russians, and when I started to skate in August, I was certain I'd be ready to play in Moscow.

"But my knees got worse instead of better. I'd skate with Team Canada in practice and the knee would swell up after the workout. Once they had to drain fluid from it, and that frightened me a little. I called Dr. Rowe in Boston and he told me not to be concerned, that it would get better in time.

But I still fretted about it. When I was in Stockholm with Team Canada for exhibition games before the Russian half of the series, I was walking down the street and the knee locked. I almost fell over."

Orr was extremely nervous as a spectator during the games in Moscow when Team Canada worked its amazing comeback to win hockey's unofficial "World Series."

"I'm a very poor 'watcher,'" Orr said. "I was so nervous in Moscow that I stayed in my hotel room and watched the final game on television.

"There was some criticism that I should have missed the trip to Sweden and Russia and worked out with the Bruins to get into condition. That's baloney! I worked harder with Team Canada than I would have at training camp. Karl Elieff was a Team Canada physiotherapist and he's one of the best. He worked on my knee every day."

When Orr returned to the Bruins, he discovered that the team had changed considerably. Steady forward Ed Westfall had been claimed by the New York Islanders in the expansion draft and four other Bruin regulars had defected to the new World Hockey Association. Orr's close friend Ted Green moved to the New England Whalers; goalie Gerry Cheevers shifted to the Cleveland Crusaders; Derek Sanderson and Johnny McKenzie had accepted huge contracts with the Philadelphia Blazers of the WHA.

Surprised, Orr returned to the Bruins' lineup for the fifth game of the season.

"Everybody knew I wasn't ready to play, especially me," he said. "But I had to find out for myself. I found out very quickly that there were many things I couldn't do on the ice, like pivot on my skates. The knee really bugged me, and the doctors said my being overweight (by ten pounds) was too much of a load for the left leg to carry.

"After a few games, management, the doctors, and I

agreed that I should quit for three weeks and devote all my efforts to building up the leg and knee. I skated every day for ninety minutes, rode ten miles on the exercise bike, and worked out several hours in a gymnasium. I watched my diet very carefully, and in those weeks I took off all the excess beef. My leg and knee strengthened to the point where I felt I could take a regular shift."

The situation in the East division of the NHL had changed drastically because the Bruins no longer were the overwhelming powerhouse club. The Montreal Canadiens had assumed that position as top team, anchored by the great goaltending of Ken Dryden. When Orr rejoined the Bruins on November 18, they trailed the Canadiens by 14 points.

"When a team loses five regulars, every guy on the club has to be a little bit better," Orr explained. "In the early part of the '72–73 season, we just weren't hungry. Before that we had extra talent all over the place. Losing those guys meant that we just had talent, not extra talent, and everyone had to work that much harder to compensate."

With typical modesty Orr laughed off any mention that the Bruins' slow start was the result of Number 4 not being in top form. However, when he rejoined the team in November, Orr quickly established the extent of his value to the Bruins. He scored 7 goals in his first 8 games, and the Bruins reduced the Canadiens' lead from 14 points to 4.

The Bruins' pursuit of the Canadiens was fruitless. The team was plagued by ordinary goaltending and the inexperience of serveral young players. Early in the season Harry Sinden, who had coached the team to the 1970 Stanley Cup and was the manager-coach of Team Canada, returned to Boston as the managing director of the Bruins, in complete charge of the hockey operation.

In late January, when the Bruins were in danger of losing

second place to their archrivals, the New York Rangers, easygoing Tom Johnson was removed from the coaching job. His replacement was volatile Armand "Bep" Guidolin, who had coached the Boston Braves, the Bruins' farm team in the American League.

"The team's problems certainly weren't Tom's fault," Orr said. "All the players liked him a great deal. We just didn't work hard enough and because of that, Tom was fired."

Guidolin's hard-driving approach boosted the Bruins to a strong finish, in which they held off the Rangers to take second place. But they were 13 points inferior to the Canadiens in the final standings.

Orr participated in 63 games and produced 29 goals and 72 assists for 101 points. He finished third in the scoring race behind his mate Phil Esposito, who compiled a 55–75–130 point total, and Bobby Clarke of the Philadelphia Flyers.

Although Orr's statistical achievements indicated a very fine season, his play was affected noticeably by his knee troubles. He was unable to pivot properly, especially to his right, when skating backward. That forced him to modify the flat-out rushing style of his early NHL years. In the view of many rivals Orr's new conservative style made him even more dangerous.

The Bruins were paired against the Rangers in the quarter-final series of the Stanley Cup play-offs. The close-checking Rangers, inspired by their frequent losses to the Bruins, played excellent defensive hockey to win the best-of-7 series, 4–1. Any hope the Bruins had of winning vanished in the second game when Esposito sustained a knee injury that required surgery to repair.

Although Orr claimed the 1972–73 season was one he wanted to forget, there were assorted positive factors. In late January Orr's engagement to Margaret "Peggy" Wood, a petite, blond schoolteacher from Detroit, was announced. Thus, the most eligible bachelor in the sport was removed from the list.

In the winter of 1973, Orr's lawyer and closest friend, Alan Eagleson, began negotiations with the Bruins on a new contract for the superstar defenseman, although Orr's old contract didn't expire until the conclusion of the 1975–76 season.

In addition to dealing with the Bruins, Eagleson also contacted all WHA teams to inquire if they were interested in making an offer for Orr's services when his Bruins pact ended.

"Bobby's next contract certainly will be the largest, most complex deal in the history of the sport and we wanted to get an early start at it," Eagleson said. "Our contacting the WHA teams didn't indicate that we were thinking of Bobby changing teams, because he's never wanted to play anywhere but Boston. It's just that a WHA team might have an interesting proposal."

Rumors claimed that Eagleson's proposals for Orr's new contract with the Bruins included a salary of at least $500,-000 per season. A WHA team, the Minnesota Fighting Saints, quickly answered Eagleson's inquiry. The Saints said they were very interested in Orr's services.

Any mention of his financial situation always brought a somewhat embarrassed chuckle from Orr. His standard reply was: "You'll have to ask the Eagle because I don't know anything about those things. I'm just a little kid from Parry Sound and the Eagle gives me an allowance."

Orr did voice one small tongue-in-cheek complaint about his lawyer.

"Everytime the Eagle works out a deal for some player, a hotshot rookie or anyone else, it seems he always says the 'contract is bigger than Orr's,'" Bobby laughed. "I keep asking him what's going on. How come everyone else has a bigger contract than me?"

The summer of 1973 was a very relaxed one for Orr. He and Peggy spent much of the time with his parents at Parry Sound. Fishing trips on the Moon River were a summer ritual for Bobby and his father.

The news media tried every possible means to discover the date of Orr's wedding but, as always, he guarded his private life very carefully.

"The wedding will be very secret and very quiet," Orr said. "Just our families and a few close friends will be there."

On a Saturday evening in early September Robert Gordon Orr and Peggy Wood were married quietly by the Orr family minister in Parry Sound. The honeymoon was brief. The following Tuesday, Orr was at the Bruins' training camp in Fitchburg, Massachusetts, making preparations for the 1973–74 NHL season.

Hockey's two most famous knees were in prime health. A summer of hard work had Phil Esposito almost completely recovered from knee surgery, and Orr's knee was in excellent condition.

The Bruins had made some excellent off-season deals. Most important was the trade with the Minnesota North Stars, in which the Bruins acquired young goalie Gilles Gilbert in exchange for veteran center Fred Stanfield. Two impressive rookies fresh from junior hockey, defenseman Al Sims, who partnered Orr, and center Andre Savard, earned first-string berths.

The "new" style of hockey that Orr's knee problem had forced him to adopt in the 1972–73 season was perfected in the 1973–74 campaign.

"Bobby Orr is doing more now by doing less," said Toronto Maple Leaf coach Red Kelly, who was a perennial

NHL All-Star defenseman during his career with the Detroit Red Wings.

"Bobby no longer takes the physical risks he did in his earlier seasons. He's playing the way Doug Harvey did when Harvey was the best defenseman in hockey. Orr plays with great control now. He carefully calculates every move."

Harvey was the Hall of Fame backliner of the Montreal Canadiens in the 1950's about whom it was said: "He could play defense in a rocking chair." Harvey always appeared to be lazy and almost indifferent to the action around him. However, with supreme application of his skills, he became one of the game's most valuable workers. Harvey had the ability to slow down the pace of a game, lull opponents into a sense of false security, and then explode with a burst of rushing speed or a quick clearing pass to a breaking forward.

In his early NHL seasons Orr had taken some incredible physical risks. When an opponent cut off his path along the boards, Orr many times tried to hurdle over him. If two defensemen attempted to sandwich him on one of his many rushes, Orr frequently attempted to crash between them.

His physical capabilities reduced by his knee problems, Orr quickly adjusted his style to a more conservative approach. No longer did he rush the puck up the ice on just about every play. Instead he lured opposition forecheckers toward him, then passed the puck to a moving Bruin forward. Often he used his amazing puck-control ability to slow the pace of a game to a crawl, then eluded checkers with a quick burst of speed or a deadly accurate pass.

"Sure, I didn't want to risk further injuries to my legs but I'm a much smarter player now than I used to be," Orr explained. "I've discovered that you can save a lot of energy by being smart on the ice, by passing the puck more. Besides, a quick pass gets the puck from point A to point B much more quickly than I can carry it.

"Why bull your way between two defensemen yourself when you can pass the puck to a teammate, then sneak around behind the defensemen and receive a return pass? Why try to go between a guy and the boards when the odds are strongly against your making it? I'm just learning those things now."

The Bruins regained their position as the top NHL team during the 1973–74 season. They won the East division pennant by 14 points over the Montreal Canadiens. Meanwhile the amazing Philadelphia Flyers finished first in the West division with only 1 point less than the Bruins' 113, and hockey fans were excited about the prospects of a Bruin-Flyer final for the Stanley Cup.

The Orr-Esposito scoring machine again dominated the NHL statistics. Esposito won the scoring title with 68 goals and 77 assists for 145 points; Orr was runner-up with a 32–90–122 point figure.

The fans got their wish when the Bruins and Philadelphia Flyers met in the final. The Bruins eliminated the Toronto Maple Leafs and Chicago Black Hawks in early rounds to qualify for the big series against the Flyers, who had side-lined the Atlanta Flames and New York Rangers.

Under coach Fred Shero the Flyers had developed into a superior defensive team, a tight-checking, well-disciplined club. They also earned the nickname "The Broad Street Bullies" for their frequent fights and record penalty totals. They were led by center Clarke and goalie Bernie Parent.

The Bruins won the series opener, 3–2, at Boston. Orr made a big play to set up the first goal, then produced the winning score at 19.38 of the third period with a sizzling slap shot. Clarke's overtime goal gave the Flyers a 3–2 win in the second game, the Philadelphia team's first victory at Boston Garden since it entered the NHL in the 1967 expansion.

The Flyers claimed 4–1 and 4–2 triumphs at Philadelphia for a commanding 3–1 edge in the series. Pivotal in those wins were the defensive tactics the Flyers deployed against Orr. Many teams were reluctant to send players deep into the Boston zone to forecheck him because they would be trapped there when he eluded them. The Flyers often sent three forwards in to harass Orr by reducing the space in which he could maneuver.

"Bobby, of course, is the greatest player in the game and you have to be careful in how you defend him," said Clarke, the Flyers' inspirational leader. "But if he doesn't have any room to work in, his effectiveness has to be cut down."

In the fifth game at Boston Orr staged a superior individual performance to rally the Bruins. He arranged the first goal of the game on a brilliant rush, then scored twice as the Bruins stayed alive in the series with a 5–1 win. However, it seemed the Flyers were the team of destiny. Backed by Parent's incredible goaltending, they became the first expansion team to win the Stanley Cup with a 1–0 triumph in the sixth game.

As always, Orr, the superb team player, took the defeat hard.

"Give the Flyers credit," he said. "We played well, but they just wanted it more than we did."

Following the final game, Orr visited the Flyer dressing room to offer his congratulations. The Flyer players wanted him to have a drink of champagne from the Stanley Cup but Orr declined.

"Only the winners drink from the cup," Orr said.

That loss failed to detract from the widely held view that Bobby Orr is the finest player in the history of the game. At the conclusion of the 1973–74 season, his eighth in the NHL, a list of Orr's achievements supplied glowing testimony to that view.

In those 8 seasons Orr has played 541 games, scored 213 goals, and secured 522 assists for a total of 735 scoring points. His average of 1.34 points per game is the highest in NHL history.

He was an All-Star in all eight seasons, including 7 consecutive nominations to the first All-Star team. He has won the Norris Trophy as best defenseman in 7 consecutive seasons. He was named the most valuable player (Hart Trophy) 3 times and he has won the Conn Smythe Trophy as the most valuable player in the play-offs twice. He has even won the Ross Trophy as NHL scoring champion, perhaps his most incredible feat because the possibility of a defenseman leading the NHL scoring was as remote as a pitcher leading major-league baseball in home runs.

In July, 1974, the arrival of Robert Darrin Orr at Parry Sound hospital, the first child of Bobby and Peggy Orr, completed the picture for this remarkable man, athlete, and citizen.

INDEX

156

The Author

When Al Hirshberg died on April 11, 1973, American sports fans lost one of their most popular writers. Among his widely read books from Putnam's are *Frank Howard: The Gentle Giant; Baseball's Greatest Catchers;* and *Henry Aaron: Quiet Superstar.* Now Frank Orr, a well-known Canadian sportswriter, has finished this Hirshberg biography of Bobby Orr, the all-around hockey great. Frank Orr's books for Putnam's include *Hockey's Greatest Stars* and *Hockey Stars of the 70's.*